I0620201

American Civil War Stories

50+ True and Fascinating Tales of Battles, Heroes, and the People Who Changed History

Table of Contents

Introduction

The American Civil War was one of the defining moments that shaped the identity of the United States as a country. The values of freedom, justice, and equality solidified in the Constitution were extended to all people in the aftermath of the war. Where the United States finds itself today did not happen with the snap of a finger immediately after the war ended. There was still discrimination – and even today, some groups experienced forms of oppression, but the Civil War got the ball rolling to introduce the populace to a fairer world.

The ideals of the United States were worked out on the battlefield as one group fought to end slavery, and another wanted to uphold the discriminatory practice because their livelihood depended on it. The complex mix of cultural identity, state rights, and liberation for all people resulted in floods of blood on the grounds of the country, which paid the debt for the life that modern Americans enjoy.

Exploring the history and stories of the Civil War gives you a glimpse into the past and reveals how trailblazers can change how society functions. The revolutionary spirit of those who fought against oppression to create a new future for America lives on in the records of history. Digging deeper than the surface level and unpacking the details of key moments, ideas, and people in the Civil War period brings this often-neglected moment to life.

The Civil War unveils the darkest and brightest parts of human beings. The paradox of civilization is that you often must dive into the deepest crevasses of war, bloodshed, turmoil, and oppression to rise to the highest heights of righteous values and prosperity. As you go through this book – taking a walk through the battlefields and homes of the brave and cursed souls of the Civil War – you awaken to the reality that if you do not know the darkness of the past, you are doomed to repeat it in the future. Moreover, those who stood courageously against injustice should be elevated as models for the modern world to emulate.

From the first bullet fired to the healing and reconciliation process and everything in between, this conflict will be brought to life in a way you've never experienced before. The competing ideologies and the soldiers who laid down their lives for what they believed in will be resurrected to tell the stories of the war that shaped the United States. Brace for impact as you are thrown into this world-defining period, and open yourself to the many lessons you will inevitably learn by studying the American Civil War.

Chapter 1: Heroic Tales of the Early Civil War: Brave Soldiers of 1861

The first section of this opening chapter shares the stories of individuals who eagerly enlisted in the Union and Confederate armies. The next one describes the initial skirmishes and battles of 1861, including the Battle of Bull Run (Manassas) and the Battle of Wilson's Creek. The third one highlights specific instances where soldiers displayed extraordinary bravery in the heat of battle and received achievements, including the Medal of Honor for their actions in 1861.

The fourth narrative explores the daily lives of soldiers in camp, their hardships, the grueling marches amid harsh weather conditions, and other challenges. The last story talks about lesser-known soldiers whose contributions were heroic but did not receive widespread recognition.

The Recruitment Begins

From the beginning of the war until mid-1862, recruitment for military services was voluntary-based.

From the beginning of the war until mid-1862, recruitment for military services was voluntary-based. Most enlistees were either recruited or heard about the possibility of joining the war at community meetings or by word of mouth through friends and family. During the spring and summer of 1861, masses of men of various ages joined the military. Their reasons for enlisting varied from seeking adventure or steady employment to an opportunity for an achievement that would kick-start their aspired political career. Some of them were simply driven by a duty for their country or felt the need to follow friends or family members who had already joined the service. For instance, Alonzo Ameli, a 5th New York Infantry Regiment soldier, expressed his great desire to support Northern patriotic causes in his letters home.

While not all eagerly awaiting to fight were accepted (some due to their age, others because of their ethnicity), the ranks of those who initially joined grew steadily. From those enlisted, not everyone understood the severity of the situation, with some believing the war would be over in a couple of months or by the Christmas holidays at the latest. An even more pressing problem was that the majority of the people who answered the recruiting efforts were young men without military training, coming from rural areas (especially on the Confederate side). Many new enlistees in the Confederate army only joined out of fear of a Northern invasion and weren't invested in the Southern cause. This was partially because Confederate recruitment consisted mostly of issuing warnings of possible confiscation of properties by the Northerners and causing harm to the Southern families. Those who enlisted on the other side didn't fare much better either. As the forces continued to mobilize, untrained Union soldiers defended territory they didn't know and relied on the locals for supplies and information. Neither side imagined the destruction the war would bring or that it would last for four years.

The numbers grew on both sides. For some enlistees, deciding which side to join wasn't easy - they had to weigh in devotion to the cause, family ties, past loyalties, and much more. In his letter to his cousin, Robert E. Lee details his dilemma of which side to support. While not native to Virginia, Lee developed a strong devotion to the state, and ultimately, he remained with it, supporting it through his military service.

Others without American roots also joined the army on both sides. In the Union Army, 25% of the recruited soldiers were Irish, German, and English immigrants. Yet, they were just as eager to support a cause as the Americans, and they fought for either supporting or abolishing slavery just as bravely. The new enlistees began training either in old or new artillery, infantry, and cavalry units, but they didn't get the chance to fully prepare when the first serious conflict arose.

The First Conflicts Arise

The First Battle of Bull Run (or the Battle of Manassas) was the first major squish between the two sides. As a prelude to this conflict, the Union army was under massive pressure to advance toward Richmond and get there before the Confederate Congress meeting was planned here for July 20, 1861. Stoked by the Union Army's early victories in Virginia, the press and the public in the North couldn't wait until their soldiers made another blow to the enemy. Adhering to the growing pressure, President Lincoln sent Brigadier General Irvin McDowell toward Richmond with instructions to launch a surprise offensive that would bring the war to an end. With 35,000 ill-prepared Union soldiers under his command, General McDowell marched from Washington and approached the federal capital cautiously (in fact, if it had been up to him, he would have postponed the attack until the troops received more training). Due to Lincoln's argument that the rebel armies were just as unprepared, McDowell had no other choice but to begin the offensive. However, his overly cautious actions cost him. The Confederate army learned about the Union troops' movement through their Washington espionage network and began to prepare themselves. Led by General P.G.T. Beauregard, 20,000 Confederate soldiers settled in their campsite near Manassas Junction (at the river Bull Run) and were joined by 11,000 rebels from the Shenandoah Valley, led by Confederate General Joseph E. Johnston. The two Confederate troops met at Manassas, where they would clash with the Union soldiers on the morning of July 21, 1861.

McDowell's troop delivered the first blow to the enemy and planned to surround the Confederate army by crossing the river and attempting to flank them. For the first two hours, the 10,000 soldiers on the first line were pushing back the rebels' lines, much to the onlookers' happiness (reporters, commoners, and even politicians from Washington traveled to witness what they believed to be an easy victory). However, their celebration was premature as reinforcement on the other side arrived. From then on, a series of attacks and counterattacks ensued, and the Federals continued to struggle to coordinate attacks with untrained men in all regiments. Johnston and Beauregard sent for more reinforcement, and soon, there were many more rallying by the Confederate side than the Union supporters had previously anticipated.

By mid-afternoon, both sides had equal numbers on the battlefield, and after fighting defensively for several hours, Beauregard switched tactics and launched an offensive across the enemy lines. The Confederate soldiers were eager to attack, shouting "rebel yell" as they moved forward quickly. It didn't take them much time to break the Union line, much to the letter's surprise. The confused Union soldiers began to retreat mid-chaos, crossing the Bull Run river, but were slowed down by their civilian supporters who were forced to abandon their picnic sites and run towards the field on the east.

Their victory and their shocked enemy's chaotic retreat toward Washington gave the Confederate supporters much confidence, showing the North that they couldn't count on an easy victory. During this first Battle of the Bull Run, the Confederates suffered 1,750 casualties, while the Union army lost over 3,000 men. Unfortunately, their troops were too disorganized to take advantage of the situation and attack the retreating enemy, who managed to flee to Washington. Their hope for pulling off a victory of their own was short-lived. Soon, both sides had to face the reality that the conflict had just begun and many more battles were to come.

Another major clash between the two sides was the Battle of Wilson's Creek. It included a skirmish between a Union unit of a little over 5,000 soldiers, led by General Nathaniel Lyon, and two Rebel armies with a combined force that was double Lyon's fleet. The Rebels, led by Generals Ben McCulloch and Sterling Price, met the Union soldiers in Springfield, Missouri. Despite having a poorly trained and ill-equipped troop, both Confederate commanders were willing to go ahead with the fight. General Lyon wasn't deterred by the size of enemy ranks either and made plans to attack on August 10, 1861. He led the majority of the men into a surprise attack at dawn and sent a little over 1,000 soldiers, led by General Franz Sigel, to flank the enemy and attack from the rear. His surprise attack worked, quickly sending the Confederate soldiers into a frenzy as they tried to get their bearings on their campsite. However, Siegel was surprised by another Rebel regiment, who pushed his men back, and soon the tide turned against the Union soldiers. General Lyon was killed by the Confederates, but his army managed to maintain their lines, and the Confederates soon withdrew from the battle. Still, with heavy losses and low ammunition, the Union fleet would have been at a serious disadvantage in case of a further attack. They, too, were forced to retreat to Springfield, and soon after, the Confederate army secured Southwestern Missouri.

Displaying Extraordinary Bravery

Despite being unprepared for attacks, soldiers on both sides displayed extraordinary valor and courage.

https://commons.wikimedia.org/wiki/File:General_Thomas_Jonathan_%27Stonewall%27_Jackso n_by_James_Reeve_Stuart.jpg

Despite being unprepared for attacks, soldiers on both sides displayed extraordinary valor and courage. One of these soldiers was Stonewall Jackson, a seasoned military man who left his position as a teacher to join the war. Jackson began his military career in 1842 by entering training, and after graduation, he fought in the Mexican War as a Lieutenant. After earning a reputation for his bravery and resilience in the wake of bloody battles, he rose to the rank of Brevet Major. He retired and became a teacher in 1851, but 10 years later, he was back to reinforcing the military, at first, in the Union ranks. However, after his home state, Virginia, seceded, he switched sides and began supporting the Confederacy. In mid-July 1861, serving under General Joseph E.

Johnston, Jackson (now a Brigadier General) was among the soldiers sent for reinforcement against the impending Union attack at the Bull Run River. In an incredibly heroic act, Jackson led his men into the battle to close the gap in the Confederate line before the Union soldiers could take advantage of it and use it to break the line. As they arrived, they were noted by General Barnard Bee, who told his men to take the example of this brave soldier, who was facing the enemy standing on the line like a "stone wall." This unusual nickname that was born in anticipation of the battle stuck, and Jackson became known as Stonewall Jackson from then on. For his arrival and action at this key moment (which allowed the Confederates to gain a significant strategic foothold), Jackson was later promoted to major general and received the Medal of Honor.

The acts of the other recipients of the Medal of Honor were just as heroic. For example, Artillery Commander Adelbert Ames refused to leave his battery and seek medical assistance despite being severely wounded on July 21, 1861. On the same day, on the First Battle of Bull Run, Private Abiather J. Knowles displayed extraordinary heroism when he, accompanied by only a handful of his comrades, scoured the still-under-fire battlefield, looking for and removing the wounded and the dead. Meanwhile, First Lieutenant Charles J. Murphy was on a similar mission when his regiment was pushed back, and he took on not only fighting in the ranks but also caring for the wounded on the field, which led to his falling into captivity.

Nothing shows more the importance of the First Battle of Bull Run than the fact that several officers went on to fight without being under a service contract (as the service was still voluntary at the time). Despite his contract having expired, Captain Walter H. Cooke joined Colonel David Hunter and participated in the fight as a much-welcomed aid. Two days before, Corporal James E. Cross, accompanied by only one of his comrades, voluntarily faced the enemy on the frontline of his regiment despite being severely overpowered and ordered to retreat.

On August 10th, 1861, Army Private Nicholas Bouquet abandoned the heavily reinforced line of battle to capture a horse and ride it to a disabled gun the enemy was about to capture. Despite being under heavy fire, he was able to save the gun from being seized by the enemy forces.

On September 3rd, 1861, Private Michael Madden dragged a wounded fellow soldier to the riverbank while under enemy fire, jumped into the river, and swam to the safety of the Union lines, all while holding onto his comrade. In an incredibly courageous act, Army Musician George H. Palmer volunteered to join the trenches and not only fight but lead a charge toward the enemy. His actions on this mid-September day helped the Confederate sharpshooters recapture a Union hospital and gain a military foothold in the region.

On November 7, 1861, a severely wounded Union Navy Captain named George H. Bell remained on the frontline and displayed extraordinary courage, saving many of his comrades' lives during a painful battle.

Daily Life in the Battle Camps

While the Civil War was marked by the most vicious battles in U.S. history, the soldiers in the battle camps spent most of their time either training or marching. Arranged in a grid pattern (with streets between the grids), army camps had different units across the numerous grids, with new enlistees positioned toward the rear and officer quarters toward the front. The soldiers' days were marked with monotony, beginning at 5 in the morning with a drill, followed by another drill, and then several more drills, one after another, until the day ended.

This meant that the first drill began before breakfast. After this, the Union soldiers had a modest meal consisting of a hardtack (a biscuit made from flour and water), while the Confederate army had dried meat, cornbread, and beans for breakfast. However, because of food shortages, the meat and beans for the Confederate soldiers were not always available, and if they wanted to have a filling meal, they would have to hunt and forage for the ingredients. Neither side was supplied with vegetables and fresh fruit, which meant that their diet lacked vitamins and other essential nutrients, and the soldiers often suffered from scurvy.

Moreover, clean water was also in short supply for drinking and bathing. By being forced to drink contaminated water, the soldiers were exposed to other diseases, including dysentery. Due to the lack of bathing practices, the camps were permeated with a heavy smell from a combination of sweat, blood, animal odor, and food.

The drills included practicing shooting (for new enlistees) and specific maneuvers (for trained officers). When not doing a drill, soldiers gathered wood, dug trenches, cleaned, and searched for water.

Housed in crowded canvas tents, up to 20 Union soldiers shared a space meant for 12. Their bedding was infested with lice, which made the arrangement even more uncomfortable. However, the Confederate soldiers had it even worse. Due to a serious canvas shortage, the men were forced to sleep on piles of leaves between logs or on straw pellets when those were available. When the winter arrived, Confederate soldiers took it upon themselves to build wood huts to survive the harsh conditions. Several hospital tents were also on both sides of the numerous soldiers' dwellings.

To find some diversion from the monotonous life in the camps, soldiers played card games, had boxing matches, gambled, and were entertained by either army musicians or talented instrument players among the regular members. Those with family waiting at home often spent their time writing letters about the events in the battles or describing their life in the camps. In his letter to Reverend Alexander E. Thompson, a soldier named Johnnie describes his life at Camp Parapet as boring and tiring and a march he was sent on with his unit at the beginning of winter 1861 as grueling. He said in his letter that he spends most of his days foraging and burning wood for meals or else doing drills.

The Unsung Heroes and Young Volunteers

Beyond the Medal of Honor recipients, many young soldiers contributed to both causes during the Civil War. For example, when 16-year-old college student James Billingslea Mitchell learned about the war's outbreak from his father, a landowner in Alabama, he transferred from the University of North Carolina to the University of Alabama, where he could start military training. By the time he turned 17, Mitchell was a drill master for the Confederate recruits, and he entered his first military campaign before he was even allowed to do it legally. Between the ages of 17 and 18, Mitchell served as a Lieutenant in the 34th Alabama Regiment, and he showed incredible bravery in numerous battles from 1861 onward despite being severely wounded several times.

Another unsung hero of this war was Andre Cailloux, a mixed-race former slave who, when the war broke out, served in the Native Guard. After his unit was disbanded, he joined the Union Army. While his new unit was mostly in charge of fatigue duty (trench digging, wood chopping, etc.), Cailloux gained the respect of his commanding officers early on for his unrelenting passion for this intense manual labor.

William Augustus Bowles (nicknamed Gus), from Uvalde, Texas, was a young boy of 13 when the war arose. His father joined the army immediately, leaving Gus in charge of the family. However, after seeing Confederate soldiers camping outside their homes soon after his father's departure, Gus told his army that he wanted to join the army, too. According to the interview he gave many years later (when asked to recount the events), Gus told a reporter that he immediately left his home and found his father's unit in Houston. He had to walk 16 miles to get there, take a train, and then walk another two miles. While surprised to see him, his father agreed to talk to his Colonel and ask if they would recruit Gus. The Colonel couldn't sign him up due to his age, but he agreed to let him stay there in his father's place while the older Bowles went home. Gus recalls spending two to three months guarding prisoners and living on starvation rations. They had no coffee as they were told it had all been tied up in the north. After a brief (and false) notice of the war's possible end, the Colonel declared they had to fight at Galveston. After only three months of training, young Gus had his first taste of battle as he found himself on the battle line facing guns. Despite experiencing copious amounts of fear, Gus showed incredible courage by taking out his own gun and getting ready to shoot.

Chapter 2: Untold Tales from 1862: Ordinary Americans in Extraordinary Times

The Civil War divided the country and led to brothers, sisters, and family members fighting one another. It was a very trying time for the American people, civilians, and soldiers alike. However, history usually focuses on the battles and the main events that took place during the war but rarely mentions ordinary people and their sacrifices and contributions to their country. While many Americans suffered during the Civil War and struggled to make ends meet, others stepped up and played crucial roles during the war.

This chapter sheds light on the suffering of the American people while also telling the story of its unsung heroes.

America in 1862

The Civil War had taken its toll on the country, leaving the people reeling and desperate for a peaceful resolution.

https://commons.wikimedia.org/wiki/File:Batalla_de_Puebla,_5-5-1862,_Constantino_Escalante_(1862).jpg

In 1862, the U.S. was extremely different from the America you know today. The Civil War had taken its toll on the country, leaving the people reeling and desperate for a peaceful resolution. That year was also crucial as the battles fought determined the war's outcome. The Union was advancing, and the North's morale was very high. They achieved many victories in the West; however, they had a rough start.

From 1861 till the beginning of 1862, neither army was able to gain the upper hand. The Civil War was unlike any war. Both sides were from the same country; many knew each other personally, and some even grew up together. Most Union and Confederate army leaders had the same background and military education and even served together. They knew each other so well that they could anticipate the other person's moves and strategies.

Many battles were fought in 1862. The Confederates achieved early victory in the Seven Days Battles, even though 20,000 of their men were either wounded or killed. However, things changed in the Battle of Antietam, which is described as one of the bloodiest battles in American history. Twenty-three thousand men lost their lives on both sides, and ended with the Union's victory.

This unexpected victory prompted Lincoln to pass the Emancipation Proclamation on September 22, 1862, which declared the freedom of all slaves in the Confederate states. Understandably, the South was furious at what they believed was a huge injustice. They attacked Lincoln in the press and accused him of trying to stir things up in the South. Interestingly, this proclamation didn't apply to the northern states.

Another influential battle in 1826 was the Battle of Shiloh, which brought another victory to the North and shattered all the South's dreams of preventing the Union from taking over Mississippi.

While the battles between the North and the South were heating up, the civilians on both sides were paying the price. The war had a devastating impact on the American people. Properties were destroyed, fences burned, there was a food shortage, churches and schools were closed, and houses turned into hospitals. People were suffering from drought and starvation. Some were forced to leave their homes to find food and water, while others had no choice but to stay put. Both faced hardships and unpredictable fates.

In this chapter, you will discover all the challenges civilians faced during the Civil War. It also sheds light on ordinary Americans' lesser-known stories and experiences during this pivotal year.

The Challenges of Civilians during the Civil War

It isn't only the soldiers who suffer at the frontlines during wars... the civilians pay a hefty price as well. During the Civil War, infrastructure was destroyed. The economy was suffering since trade was disrupted and agriculture declined due to drought. There was a severe shortage of all necessities, including food. People had to get by with what little they had. Others were begging for food in the streets.

As a result of the economic struggle, the Confederate and the Union printed money to fund the war, causing inflation in the whole country. Prices for services and goods increased drastically, and people couldn't afford their basic needs.

The occupied states that were under the control of the Union or Confederate forces suffered the most. They confiscated the civilians' properties, food, and anything they could get their hands on, leaving them to fend for themselves. The troops were also in every corner of the occupied cities, disrupting the people's daily lives. They faced many restrictions, like curfews and searches. They were even forced to work, do their laundry, and cook for the troops.

The American people became refugees in their own country. They had to escape and find safety to protect themselves and their children. Many had nothing to pack in their bags and fled with the clothes on their backs. It was one of the worst humanitarian crises America had ever seen.

Since most of the men were fighting the war, the refugees were mainly women and children. They had no financial support and had to be the breadwinners in their families. When the situation became dire, and they left their homes, many had nowhere to go. They had to resort to asking strangers to stay with them, hoping they would be kind enough to take them in and give them a home. Sadly, this story didn't have a happy ending. When the war was over, most of the refugees couldn't return home and were forced to start over in unfamiliar places.

Although many Americans welcomed the refugees into their homes, they struggled to financially support them. These communities were already suffering due to the war, and the arrival of large numbers of civilians proved more than they could handle.

The Civil War refugee situation had a huge impact on America that still echoes to this day.

The Role of Women in the Civil War

Women played pivotal roles in every part of history, and the Civil War was no different. The contributions of women during those troubling times were hard to ignore. Many took the role of their absent spouses and became farmers, factory workers, and even soldiers.

In the North, women supplied the soldiers with clothing, food, and even money. They cooked, baked, and planted vegetables and fruits for them. They also washed and sewed their uniforms and organized fundraisers to raise money for the soldiers' medicine and other needs. However, this wasn't enough for many courageous women who wanted to do more for their troops. They also worked as nurses on the frontlines, helping injured and sick soldiers and making sure the rest of the troops were in perfect health to be able to continue fighting. The federal government supported them by creating the United States Sanitary Commission to protect the soldiers from diseases and provide them with sanitation and healthy food.

Almost 20,000 women were involved with the Union War Effort and the United States Sanitary Commission. White and African-American women worked side by side as nurses, matrons, cooks, and laundresses.

The women in the South were no different. They weren't any less resilient even though they didn't have as much money or resources. They worked as cooks and nurses and wrote letters to the soldiers to raise their morale. Interestingly, many Confederate women didn't get their hands dirty and let their female slaves do all the work for them.

The Soldiers in the Civil War

One can't talk about the Civil War without mentioning the brave soldiers who sacrificed themselves daily. About 620,000 men died during the war, and each had a family and a story that was cut too short. There is no denying that the soldiers faced many struggles and hardships. Some didn't live to tell their stories, while others returned with their wounds hidden deep inside and were forced to spend the rest of their lives reliving what they witnessed on the frontlines.

The Words They Left Behind

Many of the soldiers' diaries and the letters they wrote to their friends and families have survived and given a glimpse of their experience on the frontlines.

Parker's Letters to His Siblings

One of the most popular soldiers was Ely S. Parker, whose experience in the war was no different than that of all the other soldiers. In one of his letters to his brother, Nic, he expressed his shock and grief to find that their father was dying. He learned the sad news from his sister in a previous letter. Parker was heartbroken to find that his father wasn't recovering and he wouldn't see him again.

"If he is indeed gone from among us, it is a great loss. We are orphans, scattered far and wide across this country."

One of the biggest tragedies of the war was the soldiers who lost their loved ones without getting the chance to say their goodbyes.

However, another letter showed a turn of events and that his father recovered. Parker expressed joy to his sister to learn that his father was improving. Sadly, however, Parker wasn't feeling well. It isn't clear in his letter if he was sick or injured, but he told her he was recovering slowly because he was always on duty.

Ballou's Love Letter

Major Sullivan Ballou was another soldier who became famous after he wrote a beautiful and heartfelt letter to his wife.

"The memories of the blissful moments I have spent with you come creeping over me, and I feel most gratified to God and to you that I have enjoyed them so long."

He expressed his love and gratitude for the beautiful years he shared with his wife, hoping he would share more with her and watch their sons grow up together. This letter is a reminder of what the soldiers left behind. They left their wives, parents, and children, and many never saw them again. Sadly, this was the case with Ballou, who died one week after sending his wife that letter.

Dr. Child's Letter to His Wife

Major and surgeon William Child talked about the hardships doctors and surgeons faced in the war in a letter to his wife.

"The days after the battle are a thousand times worse than the day of the battle. The dead appear sickening, but they suffer no pain. But the poor wounded mutilated soldiers that yet have life and sensation make a most horrid picture."

Child told his wife about the horrid scenes he witnessed at the war. For soldiers, the days of the battles were the worst, but for the medical staff, it was all the days after when they had to hear the screams of pain and tell young men that they would never be able to see, walk, or lead a normal life again. He told his wife that he believed this was a punishment from God to purify them from their sins.

Harsh Conditions on the Battlefield

The Civil War was one of the most violent wars in history. It is impossible to describe what the soldiers experienced during those trying times. They were surrounded by confusion, chaos, the smell and noise of gunpowder, and destruction and death. Since the war was extremely violent and bloody, many suffered from serious wounds. Soldiers were mutilated, lost their limbs, or suffered from life-changing wounds.

Although the soldiers used different weapons, they often engaged in hand-to-hand combat when they ran out of ammunition.

The war had a huge physical, mental, and emotional impact on the soldiers. They were exhausted, sick, and wounded from the constant fighting. Watching their fellow soldiers die and having to take the lives of other Americans had its emotional toll on many of them. They suffered from anxiety, PTSD, and depression.

Stories of African Americans in the Civil War

No one can ever deny the influential role of African Americans in the Civil War. Some fought on the battlefield, others saved wounded soldiers, and some acted as spies. Still, others fought for their freedom.

Abraham Galloway

Galloway was brave and relentless, and his only purpose was to give his people the life they deserved.

https://commons.wikimedia.org/wiki/File:Galloway_Abraham.jpg

After escaping slavery, Galloway traveled to the South to free his mother and other enslaved African Americans. He was brave and relentless, and his only purpose was to give his people the life they deserved. He became a spy for the Union. He pretended he was a slave while gathering information from the South and delivering it to the North. He formed a spy network with thousands of enslaved African Americans. He contributed to bringing the Union a step closer to victory. After the war, he was one of the first Black men to become a state senator.

Harriet Tubman

In 1862, Tubman traveled to the North to work as a nurse with newly freed enslaved people. Like Galloway, she also became a spy for the Union. She was a soldier and the first woman in the Civil War to lead a military expedition of 150 soldiers to attack Confederate troops. On their journey, they also rescued around 800 enslaved people. She and her men destroyed several plantations, dealing a huge psychological blow to the South. She was a significant asset to the Union for leading many expeditions and gathering more information than other spies.

Frederick Douglass

Douglass was the voice of freedom during the Civil War. He called for social reform and human rights. He wanted to abolish slavery and for Black people to have the same rights as White people.

He had many disagreements with President Lincoln because he didn't allow free African Americans to join the army. Lincoln was worried that this would cause clashes between Black people and racist Americans. However, since the South lost thousands of men in the war, Lincoln had no other choice but to allow African Americans to enlist in the army.

Douglass traveled nationwide to recruit Black men for the Union Army. When enslaved people saw him in his army uniform, they believed freedom was attainable.

Immigrant Soldiers in the Civil War

The immigrant soldiers also played a huge role during the Civil War. Many Italian men who fought to unite their country's southern and northern parts wanted to do the same in America. More men from Latin America and Europe pleaded to join the Civil War. Immigrants living in America were among the first responders to the call to arms. Over 25% of the Union army was immigrants.

So, why did these men fight for America? Why did they leave their families and homes to risk their lives for a strange country? The many posters found around the country at the time solved this mystery.

One German poster urged the people to fight for America, their adopted country. Another German poster encouraged the people to step up and save their country, America. Symbols were also used on French posters, like the Red Cap of Liberty, which represented emancipation.

An Irish soldier fighting for America explained his reasons to his father-in-law in a letter. He said that America was the Irish refugee from the tyranny they faced at home. He believed that fighting for America was just like fighting for Ireland. This was the case for many immigrant soldiers... America was their home, which they were willing to die for, and many certainly did.

Civilian Heroes in the Civil War

Civilians are the unsung heroes of any war. However, history only focuses on the men on the frontlines and forgets the nurses and doctors who saved lives daily.

Emily Parsons

Emily Parsons was a head nurse entrusted with treating a ship full of sick soldiers.
https://commons.wikimedia.org/wiki/File:Emily_E._Parsons_from_Woman%27s_Work_in_the_Civil_War-_a_Record_of_Heroism,_Patriotism_and_Patience_(1867)_p.273.jpg

Emily Parsons was a head nurse entrusted with treating a ship full of sick soldiers. Sadly, many died while others were suffering and helpless.

That took a toll on her mental health, but she was still adamant about helping the people. However, she was infected with malaria and became very ill. Emily only wanted to get better so she could return to helping the injured soldiers. She even said in her diary that when she got sick, she was of no use to anyone, so she needed to take good care of her health.

Dr. Mary Edward Walker

Dr. Walker volunteered to be the army's surgeon. Even though she was denied a commission, she still insisted on helping the soldiers during that tough time. She worked with the Union but often crossed the lines and risked her life to treat injured civilians. However, the Confederates arrested her and accused her of spying. She spent four months in one of the worst prisons in the country. She continued working with the Union and saving people's lives when she got out.

Amanda Akin

Amanda Akin left the comfort of her home to become a nurse with the army in Washington. While serving, she wrote letters to her sisters about the horrible things she witnessed. She said watching soldiers without limbs who were in severe pain put her in shock to the point that she forgot how to feel. The suffering and the pain were too much for her at times. Yet, she never left her post as she was stationed near the battlefield, receiving hundreds of soldiers every day. She was an angel of mercy, helping the soldiers and returning them to health.

Ordinary people become extraordinary during hard times. They risk their lives for a cause they wholeheartedly believe in and become heroes. The Civil War saw soldiers, civilians, African Americans, and immigrants fighting for different reasons. Some fought for their country, some for loyalty, and others for their right to survive. Every one of these people should be remembered as they contributed to the America of today.

Chapter 3: Stories from the Battlefields

Leaving the battlefield victorious is only accomplished by the brave, the resilient, and the courageous, who are always clear about their objectives and won't compromise no matter the cost. The American Civil War includes many stories like this, depicting acts of courage, sacrifice, and lessons to learn from. Here are a few incidents from the Battle of Gettysburg to get started.

The Battle of Gettysburg

The Battle of Gettysburg is recognized as a pivotal moment in the American Civil War.
https://commons.wikimedia.org/wiki/File:Thure_de_Thulstrup_-_L._Prang_and_Co._-_Battle_of_Gettysburg_-_Restoration_by_Adam_Cuerden_(cropped).jpg

This battle was fought from July 1 to 3, 1863, and it is recognized as a pivotal moment in the American Civil War, often considered the turning point in favor of the Union. The battle took place in and around Gettysburg, Pennsylvania. It involved the Union Army of the Potomac, commanded by General George G. Meade, and the Confederate Army of Northern Virginia, led by General Robert E. Lee.

One of the most iconic moments of the Battle of Gettysburg was Pickett's assault on the third day. The commanding General, Robert E. Lee, ordered General Pickett to charge on the enemy forces at the Cemetery Ridge. As the assault was carried out, the Confederate soldiers had no choice but to cross through open ground, leaving them vulnerable to attack. The soldiers faced massive artillery and rifle fire. The charge ended in a devastating defeat for the Confederates, resulting in heavy casualties. This failed assault marked a significant turning point in the battle and, ultimately, the war.

Another critical moment occurred at Little Round Top... a hill on the southern end of the Union line. On July 2, Union Colonel Joshua Lawrence Chamberlain and his 20th Maine Regiment repelled several Confederate attacks. In a desperate bayonet charge from the enemy, the 20th Maine held their ground, preventing the Confederates from flanking the Union position. This heroic retaliation enabled the Union to capture the left flank, turning the odds and leading to Union victory at Gettysburg.

The Battle of Gettysburg devastated the local landscape and significantly impacted the civilian population. Many residents fled their homes, seeking refuge from the intense fighting. The town itself became a field hospital, with wounded soldiers from both sides treated in homes, barns, and churches. The civilian experience was one of fear, uncertainty, and hardship as the pungent odor of gunfire, the devastating sounds of gunfire, and the marching armies disrupted their daily lives.

This battle provided a much-needed morale boost to the Union and disproved the notion of the Confederate Army being invincible. As the tides turned in the Union's favor in the battle, General Lee's advance toward the North was completely halted. Unfortunately, the gruesome battle left a high number of casualties on both sides, with estimates ranging from 46,000 to 51,000 killed, wounded, or missing. The victory in the battle stopped the Confederate invasion of the North and laid the foundation to deploy offensive tactics. Gettysburg is remembered as a critical moment that turned the tide of the Civil War in favor of the Union, although the conflict would continue for nearly two more years.

Key Events

July 1, 1863 (Day 1)

Engagement at McPherson's Ridge

It started with a clash between Confederate forces under General A.P. Hill's command and Union forces led by General John Buford. This initial engagement occurred at McPherson's Ridge and escalated into a larger conflict.

Union Retreat to Cemetery Hill

The early successes of the Confederate forces pushed the Union army to retreat. With his commanding army, General John Buford strategically retreated to Cemetery Hill, a solid defensive position to the south of Gettysburg. The decision to hold this high ground proved crucial as the battle unfolded, allowing the Union to ward off incoming assaults.

July 2, 1863 (Day 2)

Fighting for Devil's Den

Intense fighting occurred around Devil's Den and the adjacent Little Round Top. Union forces, including the 20th Maine, under Colonel Joshua Lawrence Chamberlain, repelled Confederate attacks. The defense of Little Round Top enabled the Union to secure the left flank and claim victory.

The Peach Orchard

Fierce fighting took place in the Peach Orchard and the Wheatfield, with both sides exchanging control of these critical positions multiple times. The struggle for these areas was part of the larger Union defensive line.

Culp's Hill and Cemetery Hill

While the majority of the fighting occurred on the Union's left and center, Confederate forces also attacked Culp's Hill on the right. Despite initially being pushed back, Union forces managed to reinforce and hold their ground.

July 3, 1863 (Day 3)

Pickett's Charge

The battle's climax occurred on the third day, with Pickett's Charge. General Robert E. Lee ordered a massive assault on the center of the Union line, specifically aiming for the high ground at Cemetery Ridge. The Confederate forces faced devastating artillery and rifle fire, resulting in a failed charge and heavy casualties.

Cavalry Action at East Cavalry Field

While less well-known than Pickett's Charge, a significant cavalry battle occurred on the Union's right flank at East Cavalry Field. Union cavalry, led by General David Gregg, repelled Confederate cavalry attempts to flank the Union's position.

The Battle of Gettysburg resulted in staggering casualties, with estimates ranging from 46,000 to 51,000 killed, wounded, or missing. The scale of the bloodshed underscored the ferocity of the conflict. The Union victory at Gettysburg marked a turning point in the Civil War. General Lee's failed invasion of the North was a significant setback for the Confederacy, boosting Union morale and dispelling the myth of Confederate invincibility.

President Abraham Lincoln delivered the Gettysburg Address on November 19, 1863, at the dedication of the Soldiers' National Cemetery. In this brief but powerful speech, Lincoln emphasized the principles of equality and democracy, framing the sacrifice of the soldiers as a dedication to preserving the Union and its ideals.

The Vicksburg Campaign

During the American Civil War, the Vicksburg Campaign was a pivotal military operation conducted by the Union Army and led by Major General Ulysses S. Grant. The campaign's primary objective was to capture Vicksburg, a vital Confederate stronghold situated on the bluffs overlooking a hairpin turn in the Mississippi River. Control of Vicksburg was strategically significant as it served as a linchpin in the Confederate supply line, providing access to the Mississippi River and facilitating the movement of troops and supplies between the eastern and western theaters of the war.

Strategic Importance

Vicksburg's location allowed it to control traffic on the Mississippi River... a key transportation route for both military and civilian purposes. The city's occupation by Confederate forces hindered the Union's efforts to gain control of this critical waterway.

The capture of Vicksburg was a crucial step in implementing the Union's Anaconda Plan... a strategic concept devised to strangle the Confederacy economically and militarily. The plan involved blockading Southern ports and gaining control of the Mississippi River to split the Confederacy in two. Capturing Vicksburg would sever the Confederate communication and supply lines along the river, isolating Confederate forces in the western theater from those in the east. This strategic isolation would weaken the Confederacy by limiting its ability to reinforce and resupply its armies.

Hardships Faced by Union Soldiers during the Siege

The Siege of Vicksburg, lasting from May 18 to July 4, 1863, was characterized by a series of intense battles and a prolonged period of trench warfare. Union soldiers encamped around the city faced a multitude of challenges:

Trench Warfare

Unable to make significant headway against the well-fortified Confederate positions, Union forces resorted to trench warfare. Extensive networks of trenches and earthworks were constructed, creating a complex and challenging battlefield. Soldiers lived and fought in these cramped, unsanitary conditions, enduring the physical and psychological toll of trench warfare.

Disease and Malnutrition

The blockade on Vicksburg resulted in shortages of food and medical supplies, affecting civilians and soldiers within the city. Malnutrition and diseases, such as dysentery and typhoid, spread rapidly among the besieged Confederate forces. Union soldiers facing similar scarcities and unsanitary conditions also suffered from these health challenges, further complicating the already difficult siege.

Emotional Toll

The siege, with its prolonged nature and constant threat of Confederate counterattacks, took a severe emotional toll on Union soldiers. The monotony of daily life in the trenches, combined with the anxiety of potential attacks, weighed heavily on the minds of the men. Homesickness, thoughts of loved ones, and the weariness of unending conflict contributed to the soldiers' emotional struggles.

Excerpts from Letters and Diaries

From the Diary of Private John Smith, Union Soldier

"June 10, 1863 – Another day spent in the muck and filth of these trenches. The constant digging seems never-ending. Rations are scant, and the stench of disease is overpowering. I dream of a warm meal and a quiet night's rest, but all I find is the cold, hard ground and the distant rumble of cannon fire."

Letter from Captain James Anderson to His Family

"July 1, 1863 – Our progress is painfully slow, and the enemy's resilience is matched only by our determination. Disease claims more comrades each day, and hunger gnaws at our stomachs. The men, though weary, stand tall. We understand the importance of this campaign – the key to the Mississippi is within our reach, and with it, the hope of a restored Union."

In these excerpts, you get a glimpse of the daily struggles, physical hardships, and emotional strains faced by Union soldiers during the Siege of Vicksburg. The firsthand accounts vividly portray these soldiers' challenging conditions as they fought for a strategic victory with profound implications for the Civil War.

Women on the Front Line

Nursing and Medical Care

Dorothea Dix, superintendent of Army Nurses, organized and trained women for the nursing roles.

https://commons.wikimedia.org/wiki/File:DOROTHEA_L._DIX..jpg

Women, including Gettysburg and Vicksburg, played a crucial role in supporting the wounded and providing medical care in the aftermath of the 1863 battles. Organizations like the United States Sanitary Commission mobilized women as nurses and aid workers. Dorothea Dix, superintendent of Army Nurses, organized and trained women for these roles. Notable among these women was Clara Barton, who gained recognition for her tireless efforts in caring for wounded soldiers. Following the Battle of Gettysburg, Barton and her team provided medical assistance, distributed supplies, and tended to the needs of soldiers on both sides.

Aid and Supportive Roles

Women actively participated in organizing Sanitary Fairs, which were large-scale fundraising events held in various cities to support the Sanitary Commission. These fairs featured handmade goods, artworks, and other items donated by women, with the proceeds used to purchase medical supplies and support the war effort. Women formed numerous relief organizations to aid soldiers and their families. The Ladies' Aid Societies and Soldiers' Aid Societies were prominent examples. These groups collected and distributed supplies, wrote letters to soldiers, and offered emotional support to those affected by the war.

Spies and Intelligence Gathering

Some women played covert roles as spies, gathering intelligence for their respective sides. Belle Boyd, a Confederate spy, operated in the Shenandoah Valley and provided valuable information to General Stonewall Jackson. Union spy Elizabeth Van Lew, known as "Crazy Bet," operated in Richmond, Virginia, and conveyed crucial intelligence to Union forces. Rose O'Neal Greenhow, a Confederate spy in Washington, D.C., used her social connections to gather information for the Southern cause. She played a significant role in espionage during the early years of the war.

Emotional and Moral Support

Women, often wives, mothers, or sisters of soldiers, provided essential emotional support through letter writing. These letters offered comfort, encouragement, and a connection to home for the soldiers enduring the hardships of war. They played a vital role in maintaining the morale of the troops. Women managed households, farms, and businesses in the absence of their men who were away fighting. Their resilience and ability to maintain a semblance of normalcy on the home front contributed significantly to the war effort.

Participation in Sanitary and Christian Commissions

Women's Christian Commission

The Women's Christian Commission was another organization that provided spiritual and emotional support to soldiers. Women volunteered to distribute religious literature, write letters, and offer moral guidance to soldiers on both sides. In addition to fundraising, women actively organized and staffed the Sanitary Fairs. These events generated much-needed funds and served as platforms for women to contribute directly to the war effort.

Clara Barton's Early Career

Clara Barton, born in 1821, was a pioneering nurse and humanitarian known for her contributions during the American Civil War. Before the war, she worked as a teacher and became the first female clerk at the U.S. Patent Office. Her involvement in nursing and humanitarian work began when she tended to wounded soldiers during the Baltimore Riots in 1861.

Civil War and Nursing

Barton's involvement in the Civil War escalated when she aided wounded soldiers at the Battle of Bull Run (Manassas) in 1861. Recognizing the need for organized medical assistance, she began collecting and distributing medical supplies to the frontlines. Barton's efforts were driven by a commitment to providing care and comfort to those in need.

Contributions in the Aftermath of 1863 Battles

Barton's contributions became even more pronounced after the pivotal battles of 1863, particularly the Battle of Gettysburg.

Battle of Gettysburg (1863)

Following the Battle of Gettysburg, Clara Barton and her team of volunteers played a critical role in providing medical care and relief to the wounded. She tirelessly tended to soldiers, often working on the front lines and in field hospitals. Barton's efforts extended beyond nursing; she also organized the transportation of medical supplies and facilitated communication between soldiers and their families.

Establishment of the Missing Soldiers Office

In 1865, after the war's conclusion, Barton established the Missing Soldiers Office in Washington, D.C. This office aimed to identify and document the fate of missing soldiers, helping families locate their loved ones. Barton's meticulous record-keeping and dedication earned her widespread acclaim.

Founding the American Red Cross

Clara Barton's experiences during the Civil War inspired her to advocate for establishing an organization dedicated to humanitarian aid and disaster relief. Her observations of the International Red Cross during a European trip further influenced her vision.

Formation of the American Red Cross

In 1881, Clara Barton founded the American Association of the Red Cross, which would later become the American Red Cross. The organization was modeled after the International Red Cross, and it aimed to provide assistance to those affected by disasters, both natural and man-made.

Humanitarian Efforts

The American Red Cross, under Barton's leadership, engaged in various humanitarian efforts. From responding to natural disasters to aiding in international conflicts, the organization symbolized humanitarianism and compassion. This organization still continues to play a vital role in disaster response, blood donation, and humanitarian assistance both domestically and internationally.

International Involvement

Clara Barton played a key role in the United States' adherence to the Geneva Conventions in 1882, ensuring the protection of war victims and the establishment of the American Red Cross as the national authority to carry out the principles of the Conventions.

Legacy and Impact

Clara Barton's legacy extends far beyond her contributions during the Civil War. Her tireless dedication to providing aid to those in need laid the foundation for the American Red Cross. Barton's vision and commitment to humanitarian principles have left an enduring mark on the field of relief work and healthcare.

Impact of the Emancipation Proclamation on African Americans

The Emancipation Proclamation, signed by President Abraham Lincoln on January 1, 1863, carried profound implications for African Americans on both sides of the conflict. While it did not immediately free all enslaved individuals, it was a symbolic and strategic move that reshaped the character of the Civil War. In Confederate-held territories, the proclamation declared all slaves to be free, encouraging many to escape plantations and seek refuge behind Union lines. For free African Americans in the North, the proclamation validated their status and inspired a heightened commitment to the Union cause.

Contributions of African American Soldiers to the Union Cause

The Emancipation Proclamation paved the way for forming the United States Colored Troops (USCT), allowing African American men to officially join the Union Army. These regiments played a crucial role in the war effort, challenging prevailing racist beliefs about the military capabilities of African Americans. The most famous of these regiments was the 54th Massachusetts Regiment, composed primarily of African American soldiers. Colonel Robert Gould Shaw's regiment gained national attention for its bravery during the assault on Fort Wagner in 1863. Though the attack was not entirely successful, the courage and discipline displayed by the 54th Massachusetts Regiment challenged racial stereotypes and showcased the dedication of African American soldiers to the fight for freedom.

Legacy of African American Soldiers

The contributions of African American soldiers during the Civil War left a lasting legacy. Beyond their military service, these individuals played a key role in challenging the prevalent racial attitudes of the time. Monuments and memorials, such as the Robert Gould Shaw and the 54th Regiment Memorial on Boston Common, stand as enduring tributes to the bravery and sacrifices of African American soldiers. The Emancipation Proclamation and the actions of these soldiers played a crucial role in advancing the cause of emancipation and laying the groundwork for the broader struggle for civil rights in the post-war era. The narrative of African American involvement in the Civil War is one of resilience, bravery, and a steadfast commitment to the fight for freedom and equality.

Chapter 4: 1864: Secrets of the Civil War's Final Year

In the tumultuous year of 1864, the United States found itself deeply entrenched in the throes of the Civil War, a conflict that had already raged for three years. This pivotal period witnessed a confluence of events that would shape the nation's destiny. Amid the chaos and bloodshed, a silent but crucial battleground emerged - the shadowy world of espionage. This chapter delves into the secrets of the Civil War's final year, exploring the clandestine efforts that played a decisive role in shaping the course of history.

KALEM FILMS

ISSUES OF FEB. 9 AND 11, 1910

THE CONFEDERATE SPY

A STORY OF THE CIVIL WAR

LENGTH 960 FEET

THIS WILL BE OUR BIG WEEK

We shall release **THE CONFEDERATE SPY** on February 9 and **THE FEUD** on February 11, and they are the two biggest sensations of the year —two stories of intense passion, one detailing the horrors of war and the other the vindictiveness of family quarrels in certain sections of the South.

THE CONFEDERATE SPY is a story of guerrilla warfare, of a daring deed brought to a successful issue, and of a loving wife protected from a deadly peril by a faithful old slave.

Espionage was not merely a sideshow; it was a strategic imperative for both the Confederate and Union forces.

Espionage was not merely a sideshow but a strategic imperative for the Confederate and Union forces. Gathering intelligence, sabotaging the enemy, and manipulating information became integral components of the war effort. As armies clashed on the front lines, a parallel war unfolded behind the scenes, where spies and detectives operated in the shadows, often determining the fate of battles and campaigns.

Civilian life became entwined with the covert activities of ordinary citizens turned intelligence operatives. From running safe houses to passing critical information, civilians played a vital role in the intricate web of espionage. The media, too, became a player in this clandestine drama, shaping public perception of spies and their operations. Espionage stories captured the nation's imagination, influencing not just military strategy but also the hearts and minds of the populace. This chapter aims to unravel the complexity of espionage during the Civil War, drawing attention to the distinct roles and methods employed by Confederate and Union spies.

Espionage in the Civil War

Espionage went beyond mere intelligence gathering; it became a strategic weapon the Confederate and Union forces employed to gain the upper hand. The espionage landscape was multifaceted, with Confederate and Union spies employing different roles and methods to achieve their objectives.

Confederate spies often operated within Union territories, seeking vital information on troop movements, supply lines, and military strategies. On the other hand, Union spies focused on gathering intelligence within the Confederate territories. The methods varied, ranging from traditional undercover work to innovative technology for covert communication.

The impact of espionage extended beyond the military sphere, permeating civilian life in unexpected ways. Ordinary citizens became integral to intelligence work, running safe houses and serving as conduits for critical information. This grassroots involvement demonstrated the war's pervasive influence on Americans' daily lives, blurring the lines between the frontlines and the home front.

Media coverage played a crucial role in shaping public perception of espionage. Newspapers carried sensational stories of daring spy missions, creating folk heroes out of covert operatives. These narratives entertained and served as a form of propaganda, rallying support for the war effort and glorifying the individuals engaged in espionage.

Sarah Emma Edmonds disguised herself as a man named Franklin Thompson to serve as a spy for the Union Army.

One compelling story that exemplifies the intrigue of Civil War espionage is that of Sarah Emma Edmonds, who disguised herself as a man named Franklin Thompson to serve as a spy for the Union Army. Edmonds undertook dangerous missions behind Confederate lines, gathering critical information and relaying it to Union commanders. Her story underscores the courage and resourcefulness displayed by individuals who risked everything in service of their cause.

As espionage became more sophisticated, the need for effective intelligence networks grew. Both Confederate and Union forces established intricate spy rings, with Confederate spy rings like the "Confederate Secret Service" and Union networks such as the "Bureau of Military Information," operating in the shadows. These networks facilitated the flow of information and enabled commanders to make informed decisions based on real-time intelligence.

Covert missions and espionage activities in 1864 were characterized by a series of raids, sabotage, and intelligence-gathering efforts. Confederate General John Hunt Morgan's daring raid into Union territory and Union General Benjamin Grierson's successful cavalry raids in Mississippi are just a few examples of how espionage influenced the tactical decisions made on the battlefield.

The role of codebreakers and cryptanalysts added a layer of complexity to Civil War espionage. Both sides recognized the importance of secure communication, leading to the development of elaborate codes and ciphers. The ability to decipher enemy codes became a critical skill, influencing key decisions on troop movements and military strategies.

Rose O'Neal Greenhow: A Confederate Spy in Washington, D.C.

Hailing from Washington, D.C., Greenhow was a prominent socialite and a fervent supporter of the Confederate cause. Her network of informants and audacious intelligence-gathering activities positioned her as one of the most infamous Confederate spies of the era.

Rose O'Neal Greenhow's journey into espionage began with her ardent Southern sympathies. As a widow with influential connections in Washington society, she navigated the salons and political circles of the nation's capital, creating a web of contacts that would prove invaluable to the Confederate cause. Greenhow's coded messages and discreet meetings with Confederate agents showcased her adeptness at covert operations.

One of Greenhow's notable accomplishments was her role in providing Confederate General P.G.T. Beauregard with critical intelligence during the First Battle of Bull Run in 1861. Her coded messages, concealed in seemingly innocent letters, revealed Union plans and troop movements, contributing to the Confederate victory in what would become the war's first major battle.

However, Greenhow's success did not go unnoticed. Union authorities became increasingly suspicious of her activities, leading to her eventual arrest in August 1861. Undeterred, Greenhow continued her espionage efforts while under house arrest, leveraging her charm and influence to gather information. Her arrest only heightened her notoriety, transforming her into a Southern martyr and symbol of resistance against perceived Northern aggression.

Despite her imprisonment, Greenhow's influence extended beyond the confines of her home. She managed to send coded messages to

Confederate generals, and her uncanny ability to extract information from Union officials continued. The Union authorities, recognizing the persistent threat she posed, decided to take more drastic measures. In 1862, Greenhow was banished to the Confederate states.

Greenhow's journey did not end with her banishment. In the South, she was received as a heroine, and her skills were once again employed for the Confederate cause. She traveled to Europe as a diplomatic courier, attempting to garner support for the Southern states. However, her efforts were met with limited success, and she faced financial difficulties in her final years.

Tragically, Rose O'Neal Greenhow's life took a dramatic turn in 1864 when, during a covert mission to smuggle Confederate funds from Europe, her ship ran aground off the coast of North Carolina. While attempting to reach the shore in a small boat, she drowned in the Atlantic Ocean. The woman who had once been the toast of Washington society and a key player in Confederate espionage met a watery demise, leaving behind a legacy that continued to captivate the imagination of those fascinated by the hidden world of spies.

Greenhow's story is emblematic of the complexity and risks inherent in Civil War espionage. Her ability to operate in the heart of the Union capital for an extended period showcases the challenges faced by authorities in countering covert activities. Moreover, Greenhow's charisma and resourcefulness underscore the vital role individuals with societal connections play in intelligence-gathering efforts.

The impact of Greenhow's espionage reverberated beyond her immediate circle. It inspired other Southern sympathizers to contribute to the Confederate cause through covert means, fostering a culture of intrigue and subterfuge. Her coded messages, now preserved in historical archives, stand as a testament to the ingenuity employed by spies during this tumultuous period.

Belle Boyd: Daring Confederate Spy in the Shenandoah Valley

Belle Boyd's journey into espionage was marked by a series of daring actions and a steadfast commitment to the Confederate cause.

A daring and audacious Confederate spy, Boyd's contributions to the Southern cause in the Shenandoah Valley became legendary, earning her the moniker "La Belle Rebelle." Belle Boyd's journey into espionage was marked by a series of daring actions and a steadfast commitment to the Confederate cause. Born in Martinsburg, Virginia (now West Virginia), Boyd witnessed the early stages of the war unfold in her hometown. In July 1861, at the tender age of 17, she experienced a pivotal moment that set the stage for her future espionage endeavors.

During the Union occupation of Martinsburg, Belle Boyd boldly confronted a group of Union soldiers who had entered her home. A heated exchange ensued, leading to Boyd shooting and killing a Union soldier in self-defense. This dramatic event earned her the admiration of her Southern peers and marked the beginning of her involvement in intelligence work.

Boyd's daring actions and charm became her primary tools as she engaged in espionage in the Shenandoah Valley. Operating under the guise of a flirtatious young woman, she successfully extracted valuable information from Union officers through social interactions and seemingly innocent conversations. Her ability to manipulate situations and charm high-ranking Union officers showcased her innate talent for intelligence gathering.

One of Boyd's most significant contributions occurred during the 1862 Shenandoah Valley Campaign, led by Confederate General Stonewall Jackson. Boyd intercepted critical information about Union plans, which she promptly conveyed to Confederate commanders. This intelligence was pivotal in Jackson's successful military maneuvers, earning Boyd admiration and gratitude from Confederate leadership.

Boyd's espionage activities extended beyond traditional methods. She utilized her charm and wit to infiltrate Union social circles, extracting information from unsuspecting officers. Her fearless approach and knack for seizing opportunities made her a formidable figure in the intelligence game. Boyd's activities were not confined to passive information gathering; she actively participated in shaping the course of events in the Shenandoah Valley.

Union authorities eventually caught wind of Boyd's activities, leading to her arrest in July 1862. Despite being imprisoned, Boyd's indomitable spirit persisted. She managed to maintain a defiant attitude and continued her intelligence work even from behind bars. Rather than stifling her efforts, her captivity only fueled the intrigue surrounding her.

Boyd's story became a media sensation, both in the North and in the South. Newspapers on both sides covered her arrest and subsequent imprisonment, turning her into a symbol of Southern resistance. Her intelligence exploits and her ability to defy Union authorities added to the mystique surrounding her persona.

In December 1862, Boyd was released as part of a prisoner exchange, and she returned to the Confederate fold. Her exploits continued, and she became prominent in Confederate propaganda efforts. Boyd even traveled to England and Canada on diplomatic missions, leveraging her notoriety to garner support for the Confederate cause abroad.

The post-war period saw Boyd capitalize on her wartime fame. She published her memoir, "Belle Boyd in Camp and Prison," recounting her experiences and contributing to the romanticization of her role as a Confederate spy. Boyd's life after the war included a stint as an actress, and she remained a prominent figure in the collective memory of the South.

Elizabeth Van Lew: Union Spy in Richmond, Virginia

Elizabeth Van Lew, a woman of staunch Unionist principles, defied societal expectations and operated an extensive intelligence network within the Confederate stronghold. Her contributions to the Union cause during the Civil War make her a remarkable and often overlooked figure in the annals of espionage.

Elizabeth Van Lew was born into a prominent Richmond family, and her Unionist sentiments were cultivated early in life. Despite the prevailing Confederate sympathies in Richmond, Van Lew remained steadfast in her loyalty to the Union. As the Civil War unfolded, she transformed her family home into a hub for Union intelligence gathering.

Van Lew's espionage activities were not limited to passive information collection. She actively recruited agents and sympathizers to form a covert network aimed at undermining the Confederate war effort. Her ability to maintain these connections amid the ever-watchful eyes of Confederate authorities was a testament to her cunningness and resourcefulness.

One of Van Lew's most significant contributions to the Union cause was her assistance to Union prisoners of war held in the infamous Libby Prison. Van Lew used her social connections to comfort and support these prisoners, often delivering food, medicine, and even clothing. Her compassion extended to organizing a secret escape network for Union officers, allowing them to return to Union lines.

Van Lew's residence became a safe haven for Union prisoners and sympathetic Confederate deserters. Her ability to operate in plain sight, disguised by her societal status and benevolent reputation, allowed her to continue her espionage activities undetected. The Van Lew mansion became a hub for coded messages, clandestine meetings, and a center of Unionist resistance in the heart of the Confederacy.

As Richmond faced increasing hardships due to the war's progress, Van Lew's activities became more audacious. She successfully placed her protégé, Mary Bowser, an African-American woman, as a servant in the Confederate White House. Bowser's intelligence-gathering efforts within the highest echelons of Confederate power provided Van Lew with invaluable insights.

Despite the risks, Van Lew's network expanded, and she communicated directly with Union generals, including Ulysses S. Grant. Her information proved instrumental in shaping Union military strategy in the Richmond theater. Grant later acknowledged Van Lew's contributions, referring to her as the "bravest woman" he encountered during the war.

However, Van Lew's covert operations did not go unnoticed by the Confederate authorities. Suspicion grew, and her activities became a subject of scrutiny. Despite facing increasing threats, Van Lew continued her espionage efforts, driven by an unwavering commitment to the Union and an unyielding belief in the righteousness of her cause.

In 1864, as Union forces closed in on Richmond, Van Lew's network provided crucial intelligence on Confederate defenses. When Richmond fell in April 1865, Van Lew's actions were revealed, and she faced severe backlash from her community. Her family estate was confiscated, and she was ostracized by Richmond society. Despite these hardships, Van Lew remained resolute in her convictions, highlighting the personal sacrifices borne by those engaged in espionage.

After the war, Van Lew's financial situation deteriorated, and her pleas for reimbursement from the U.S. government went unanswered. However, her story did not fade into obscurity. Van Lew's legacy was revisited during the late 19th century, and efforts were made to recognize her contributions. In 1902, the U.S. government provided financial assistance to Van Lew in recognition of her wartime service.

Covert Missions and Espionage Activities in 1864

As the Civil War entered its crucial final year in 1864, the landscape of covert missions and espionage activities evolved, reflecting the relentless pursuit of a strategic advantage by both the Confederate and the Union forces.

One notable aspect of covert missions in 1864 was the escalation of raids behind enemy lines. Confederate General John Hunt Morgan, renowned for his audacious tactics, executed a daring raid into Union territory known as "Morgan's Raid." In June 1864, Morgan led his cavalry forces into Kentucky, Indiana, and Ohio, disrupting Union supply lines, capturing prisoners, and creating panic among Northern communities. While the raid ultimately ended in defeat for Morgan at the Battle of Buffington Island, it demonstrated the potential impact of bold, unconventional actions on the war's course.

Union General Benjamin Grierson, recognized for his successful cavalry raids earlier in the war, undertook another series of raids in Mississippi in 1864. Grierson's Raid aimed to disrupt Confederate communications and supply lines, diverting attention from General William T. Sherman's Atlanta Campaign. Grierson's cavalry covered hundreds of miles, raiding and spreading confusion among Confederate forces.

Sabotage became a crucial aspect of covert operations during this period. Both sides recognized the strategic value of disrupting the enemy's infrastructure and supply network. Confederate operatives engaged in acts of sabotage against Union transportation and communication systems. Notably, the infamous Confederate spy, Belle Boyd, participated in a plot to derail a train carrying Union troops, showcasing the convergence of espionage and sabotage.

Union forces responded with their own sabotage operations, often relying on covert agents and military intelligence. The Union's efforts aimed to cripple the Southern war machine by targeting railroads, telegraph lines, and other critical infrastructure. These actions sought to create chaos behind Confederate lines, hindering their ability to effectively respond to Union offensives.

Intelligence gathering remained a constant and critical aspect of covert missions. Both Confederate and Union spies operated diligently to procure information about enemy movements, plans, and troop strength. The Bureau of Military Information (BMI), established by Union General George McClellan and later led by Colonel George Sharpe, played a pivotal role in collecting and analyzing intelligence. The BMI's efforts provided Union commanders, including General Ulysses S. Grant, with valuable insights into Confederate strategies.

The Confederate Secret Service, headed by the resourceful Captain Thomas H. Hines, continued its covert activities, attempting to gather intelligence on Union movements and plans. Hines, operating deep within Union territory, engaged in espionage and reconnaissance, highlighting the persistence of Confederate intelligence efforts even in the face of mounting challenges.

A notable incident in 1864 involved the theft of Union General Philip Sheridan's dispatch bag by Confederate spy Emeline Pigott. Using her

Southern sympathies and feminine charm, Pigott managed to seize Sheridan's bag, which contained critical documents detailing Union plans. The information she gathered was swiftly relayed to Confederate commanders, providing them with a strategic advantage.

The evolving nature of warfare also saw an increased reliance on technology in espionage. Both sides employed telegraphy and signal systems for communication, leading to the emergence of skilled codebreakers and cryptanalysts. The ability to decipher enemy codes became a valuable skill, influencing key decisions based on intercepted and decoded messages.

A notable figure in this cryptographic arena was Elizabeth Smith Friedman – a Union codebreaker and cryptanalyst. Friedman's expertise in deciphering Confederate codes contributed to the Union's intelligence capabilities. Her work, often overlooked in historical narratives, was crucial in ensuring the security of Union communications and intercepting Confederate messages.

In conclusion, in the final year of the Civil War, 1864, a clandestine world of spies, covert missions, and codebreakers played a crucial role in shaping history. From the daring exploits of spies like Rose O'Neal Greenhow and Belle Boyd to covert missions deep behind enemy lines, these hidden efforts influenced the course of battles. The silent war of codebreakers, led by figures like Elizabeth Smith Friedman, added another layer to the conflict. Deciphering enemy codes provided crucial intelligence, impacting military strategies and decisions. Together, these covert operations represented the unsung heroes who, in the shadows, left a mark on the unforgettable era.

Chapter 5: Tales of the Underground Railroad

Enslaved people led terrible lives and lived under inhumane conditions. They worked for long hours without any compensation and weren't given proper food or a comfortable place to rest at night. If they made one small mistake, they were severely punished. If they got married or had kids, their masters had the right to sell any of their family members to the highest bidder. They didn't have any other option; it was either to live as slaves or try to escape and get tortured or killed.

Many considered escaping, but they were hunted down like animals. If caught, they were executed in front of the other slaves as a lesson to anyone who was thinking of running away. Those who didn't get caught were always looking over their shoulders. If someone recognized them as a slave, they would return them to their master. Things seemed bleak for enslaved people. However, things changed in the 18th century with the arrival of the Underground Railroad.

This chapter covers the history of the Underground Railroad and tells the story of some of its most influential members and their heroic actions.

The History of the Underground Railroad

The Underground Railroad was a network of routes, places, and White and African-American spies.

The Underground Railroad was a network of routes, places, and White and African-American spies. They aided enslaved people in the Confederate states to escape to the North and offered them financial support and shelter. It wasn't an actual underground railroad... the name was more metaphorical than literal. However, the network acted as a method of transportation, moving enslaved people to safe places through canals, rivers, bays, ferries, trails, and roads. They also didn't operate underground but in churches, barns, and homes. The Underground Railroad helped enslaved people living in Maryland, Virginia, and Kentucky.

The people running this network had one purpose: freeing enslaved African Americans and helping them get the life they deserved. They were willing to risk their lives and everything they owned to free and protect enslaved people. They were farmers, ministers, or businessmen... just ordinary people who wanted to see justice prevail. Some of them were also former slaves and were risking losing their newfound freedom to help their people. Many wealthy people were also involved with the Underground Railroad, like millionaire Gerrit Smith, who would buy enslaved people and set them free.

One of the first people to help enslaved people was Levi Coffin. He started when he was only 15 years old. He would find enslaved fugitives and move them to a safe place. He was so popular among African Americans that they often sought his assistance.

Josh Brown was one of the most famous Underground Railroad conductors who helped enslaved people escape to Canada. Sadly, in 1859, he was hanged for treason. Reverend Calvin Fairbank, Captain Jonathan Walker, and Charles Torrey were other men who aided enslaved people and were imprisoned for their actions.

There isn't any information about the movement's origin. Although it was operating in the 18th century, during the Civil War, many believe it was established years before that. It started as a secret organization until its intentions became known to the Confederacy, so they started working in the light.

The first mention of the Underground Railroad dates back to 1831. A story was published about Tice Davids, who was enslaved in Kentucky and escaped to Ohio. His master was furious and blamed a movement called "The Underground Railroad" for aiding his escape. In 1839, a report was published in the Washington Post about a man called Jim, who was caught while trying to escape enslavement. He was tortured until he admitted that he was heading north to join a group called "The Underground Railroad."

In 1793, an act called the Fugitive Slave was passed, and it offered a huge reward for anyone capturing enslaved escapees, making it extremely hard for them to hide.

How the Underground Railroad Worked

Free enslaved people would send someone posing as a minister or a salesperson. They would approach an enslaved person and try to gain their trust before offering them their assistance. The Underground Railroad operator would then arrange for their escape from the plantation. However, they were usually on their own for that part, as the operator's role was only to establish contact and plan their escape.

They would then go to people called the "Conductors," who guided the enslaved people on the road and kept them safe. They hid in safe houses, which included schools, homes, and churches.

No place was safe for them in America, as anyone in the North or South could capture them and bring them back to their master for a reward. The Underground Railroad realized the safest place for them was Canada, where many of their members lived to help get the freed enslaved people started. In Canada, they were given the humane treatment they deserved. They were finally free, able to make their own choices and live the lives they wanted. They were allowed to run for office, act as jurors, and become active members of society. America tried to bring them back, but the Canadians refused.

Freedom seekers used different terminologies. They called the operators who went to find enslaved people "Pilots." People who accompanied them to freedom were called "Conductors," and enslaved people were called "Passengers." The homes and businesses where enslaved fugitives hid were called "stations."

The Civil War's Impact on Slavery

The Civil War had a huge impact on slavery. It first led to the Emancipation Proclamation, which called for freeing all slaves in the Confederate states. It encouraged many African Americans to become freedom seekers... a term describing the act of self-emancipation. These people took matters into their own hands and fought for their freedom without any outside help. There were many heroic tales of escaped enslaved people at the time, like the story of Robert Smalls.

In 1862, Smalls worked on a ship in the North. One day, its White crew left the ship to spend some time on the shore. Smalls and other enslaved people found it a great opportunity to commandeer the ship, and they went to pick up their families. Smalls posed as the ship's captain and sailed to the North with his friends and family. He hung a white flag on the ship to declare that he was surrendering and coming in peace. He even offered the ship to the first Navy captain he saw.

The North welcomed them with open arms and treated them as heroes for their courage and cleverness. Their actions showed the Union that Black men could be great soldiers. Smalls recruited 5,000 African Americans who joined the Union's army. He became a pilot and then a captain of a Navy vessel. After the war, he returned home and bought his old master's house.

Smalls' story was just one of many who succeeded in freeing themselves during the Civil War and joining the Union's fight against the Confederate states.

Harriet Tubman

Harriet Tubman was also a great leader.
https://commons.wikimedia.org/wiki/File:Harriet_Tubman_1895.jpg

You are already familiar with the heroic actions of Harriet Tubman as a nurse and as a Union soldier. However, Tubman was also one of the main conductors of the Underground Railroad.

In 1849, Harriet escaped her plantation in Maryland, along with her brothers, with the help of Underground Railroad operators. However, her brothers weren't as courageous as her and returned to slavery... perhaps they were afraid of getting caught. She went to Philadelphia, where slavery was illegal, and joined the Underground Railroad. Even though there was a bounty on her head, Tubman risked her life and returned to Maryland over a dozen times to rescue 70 of her enslaved family and friends, earning her the nickname "Moses."

Tubman preferred to go on her rescue missions during the dark winter, which gave her cover and allowed her to go unnoticed. She was one of the best conductors and never lost one person. Tubman was also a great leader. Not only did she escape slavery, but she also led many enslaved people through long and trying journeys to Canada. Her leadership skills were also apparent during her military days. She led Black and White soldiers on multiple expeditions during the Civil War.

Tubman could have spared herself all the hassle and escaped to Canada to lead a quiet and safe life. However, she refused to enjoy her freedom until all her loved ones were also free. She put her life on the line and traveled long and dangerous roads. She became an inspiration to all Black people. She once said that each person has the passion, strength, and patience to achieve anything they want and change the world.

Henry "Box" Brown

One of the most incredible escape stories is that of Henry Brown.
https://commons.wikimedia.org/wiki/File:Henry_Box_Brown_(cropped).jpg

One of the most incredible escape stories is that of Henry Brown. Born in 1815 on a Virginia plantation, Brown and his family were enslaved and sold from one master to another. He spent his childhood with his parents and seven siblings. When Brown was 15, the plantation master died, and his son took Brown to Richmond to work in his tobacco factory. This was the first time the young boy was separated from his family. Later, his siblings were also sent to different plantations.

Brown fell in love with a young slave called Nancy. They got married and had three children. Brown was a hard worker and did everything he could to make extra money to rent a house for his family. Sadly, all his dreams were shattered. While Nancy was pregnant with their fourth child, her master sold her and the children to an enslaver in South

Carolina.

Brown was devastated to be separated from his family yet again. He spent months depressed and mourning their loss. However, he decided to take action instead of being sad and feeling sorry for himself. He came up with a clever and unusual plan to escape slavery.

He went to the church and sought the help of parishioner James Caesar Anthony Smith, a free Black man, and a White man called Samuel Smith. Samuel was a shoemaker and an enslaver but agreed to help Brown for a price. The three men put their heads together to try and come up with a plan. However, they couldn't find any safe method to transport Brown.

Suddenly, Brown came up with the perfect plan. He would put himself in a box to be shipped to Philadelphia. Samuel reached out to James Miller McKim, who worked with the Anti-Slavery Society and the Underground Railroad in Philadelphia.

In 1849, Caesar and Samuel put Brown in a wooden box and sealed it. They labeled it "Dry goods" and sent it to Philadelphia. It was a long, bumpy road, and there was nothing Brown or the Smiths men could have done to prepare for what happened. The box turned to the other side, and Brown almost suffocated and died. The people transferring the box also handled it roughly, and Brown was in pain, but he couldn't scream or utter a word. It was a life-or-death situation for Brown, and he had no other choice but to endure.

After twenty-six hours, Brown arrived at the Anti-Slavery Society office. He felt as if he was brought back from the dead. However, it was all worth it as he emerged from this box a free man.

The Routes and Pathways Taken by Freedom Seekers

Since there were usually bounties on escaped, enslaved people, conductors had to be very careful. They couldn't use the same route over and over. They usually took routes from the Union states since enslavement was illegal there. For instance, Tubman took a route from the Eastern shore of Maryland to Delaware. They then either traveled to Philadelphia or Pennsylvania. Afterward, they headed further north. They usually stayed in New York or Massachusetts. Others headed farther South to Florida or Mexico and became farmers. However, some felt unsafe in America, so they traveled to Canada.

Some also took boats to Chesapeake Bay, called the "Road to Freedom." They sailed from one town to another on the bay. Others escaped by sea and took ships from North Carolina, Georgia, Savannah, South Carolina, and Charleston to Canada or other safe destinations.

Challenges Underground Railroad Workers Faced

These journeys weren't without their challenges. Some enslaved people were lucky and traveled with conductors who showed them the roads, while others didn't have maps or addresses to guide them. They memorized the routes and took tips from former slaves. Either way, the journeys were difficult and extremely dangerous. Bounty hunters and slave catchers chased them with dogs and rifles. If someone suspected them, they would either catch them for reward or alert the police. The escapees were left terrified, cold, and starving.

The Role of Safe Houses and Abolitionists

Since the routes were long, enslaved fugitives would rest in different safe houses. However, sometimes, these places were sold to slavery supporters. In that case, conductors removed them from their maps. They usually agreed with the stations' owners by word of mouth because any official documentation could endanger the enslaved people and the stations' owners.

The owners of these homes were either freed African Americans or White people who were against slavery. They risked their lives and freedom to help free enslaved people. They provided them with safe and warm homes to protect them from the cold. They offered them food, water, and shelter until they were ready to continue their journey.

Famous Abolitionists

One of the first groups of abolitionists that helped free enslaved people was called the Quakers. They were extremely influential at the time and were the main inspiration behind the Underground Railroad. One of its main members was Isaac T. Hopper... a White man who created one of the first anti-slavery networks in Philadelphia to aid enslaved fugitives. The Quakers were extremely powerful. They almost liberated George Washington's enslaved workers.

Another famous abolitionist was John Brown, who took enslaved fugitives into his home. He also created an anti-slave militia with his sons, and they freed eleven people and murdered five slave owners.

Thomas Garrett was another name that history will never forget. He always opened his home to his good friend, Harriet Tubman, and her enslaved fugitives. He aided over 2,000 enslaved people and provided them with food, clothes, money, and shelter. He even acted as a conductor and moved them to safe places.

Congressman Thaddeus Stevens was one of the biggest anti-slavery supporters, and he used his position to advocate for their freedom. He called for a law that protected African Americans and gave them equal rights. It was recently discovered that he worked with the Underground Railroad.

Blacksmith Elijah Anderson created an Underground Railroad cell in Indiana, making the state one of the most popular crossing points. He risked his life by posing as a slave owner and transporting more than 20 people at a time to safe houses.

The Significance of the Emancipation Proclamation and the 13th Amendment

The Emancipation Proclamation didn't initially have the impact everyone was hoping for, as it didn't free the slaves in the North or in the South. However, it made a huge difference in enslaved people's lives, showing them that freedom was possible. The whole world could see that one of the Union's goals for this war was abolishing slavery. Countries like France and Britain, which initially supported the Confederate states, distanced themselves from the South for their pro-slavery stance. The emancipation also allowed African Americans to join the North's army and help them win the war.

After the end of the Civil War, Lincoln realized that the proclamation had no constitutional power. Therefore, in 1865, the Senate turned it into a national policy through the 13th Amendment. It is probably one of the most significant laws in American history. It not only freed slaves, but it also prohibited the act of slavery. It was a victory for all abolitionists who had been calling for the end of slavery for years. President Abraham Lincoln was one of the law's biggest supporters.

No one was happier for that victory than African Americans. Although they didn't know what the future would hold, they experienced something they had never felt before... hope. Whatever the future held for them was better than their past and present. Enslaved people in the Confederate and Union states were overjoyed with the news.

No one can ever deny the dark history of Black America and all the terrible treatment they endured. From these dark times emerged heroes who risked everything to free enslaved people and help get them a humane life and equal rights. Black people never gave up on their freedom and did everything in their power to emancipate themselves, like Henry Brown, who almost died to become a free man. Others, like Harriet Tubman, risked their freedom to liberate their friends and families.

The Underground Railroad and the heroic actions involved will be remembered for changing America and history forever.

Chapter 6: Myths of the Civil War: Fact or Fiction (1861-1865)

History is in the eye of the beholder. Depending on whom you ask, the narrative around historical occurrences will change. Suppose you ask a defender of Confederate symbols to explain the Civil War. In that case, you will get a completely different story than if you ask a descendant of slaves. These issues of perception blur the lines between reality and fantasy. Digging through the archives of history and exploring the narrative from multiple angles will slowly reveal what is fact and what is fiction.

Digging through the archives of history and exploring the narrative from multiple angles will slowly reveal what is fact and what is fiction.

https://pixabay.com/photos/truth-lie-street-sign-contrast-257160/

To get an accurate picture of the Civil War, it is important to dispel longstanding myths that are still perpetuated today. This includes ideas about the cause of the Civil War coming from a single source or narratives that distort the disgusting attitudes of Confederate leaders about African Americans. Searching through the muddy water of history to get closer to the truth gives humanity an insight into the past that can affect how the future is shaped.

As you unpack historical narratives, the misinformation and biases of the past are revealed. Everyone has their perceptions and prejudices despite people pretending they are not present. This creates distortions, even if they are well-meaning and honest. Although it is nearly impossible to reach objectivity, you can take steps closer to it in order to gain a more accurate account of reality so that society can begin operating on well-researched and supported premises. This objective research helps prevent building the future on the shaky ground of pseudohistorical claims.

The Myth of a Simple Cause and the Reality of Complexity

Snapshot history is more about soundbites and catchphrases than actually diving deep into the truth. Boiling down the American Civil War to simply a battle over slavery is an oversimplified version of the actual complexities of the conflict. Did slavery play an important role in facilitating the war? Undeniably, yes, but it was not the only important factor to consider. Some assert that the primary cause of the Civil War was the need for States' rights, but again, this is an oversimplification. Depending on their education and biases, people will highlight one factor of many intersecting parts as the driver of the Civil War, but a broader view of the layers that led up to the war is a more accurate approach to take.

To understand how the debate around abolishing slavery first began, you must compare the economies of the North and the South. The 1800s were an excessively discriminatory time. People in the North who grew up being taught that African Americans were inferior did not wake up all of a sudden to decide to advocate for their rights and end slavery. The process that brought the culture to that conclusion was a lot more gradual and influenced by factors outside of morality and justice. The North was quickly industrializing. Northern states tend to be rather rocky, separating large sections of land. This meant that farms in the North were smaller. Furthermore, the North had harsh winters, which meant there were large parts of the year when farming was impossible. Therefore, the North developed an industrial economy that processed raw materials into more valuable goods.

The South was the opposite. Their beautiful weather year-round and large open fields meant that their economy relied on farming. So, as the North was developing cities to accommodate factories and industries, the South stuck to the plantation model, where a few people ran large sections of land using slave labor as the backbone of the workforce. The North still practiced slavery, but the institution was dying naturally because of industrialization. An industrial economy functions by processing goods so that you can add value to the raw materials. However, the agricultural economy of the South relied on the ability to produce crops cheaply, so slave labor was central to their economic model. Thus, the shifting economy of the North started to cause an initial division, with slavery coming into play in the periphery.

The less the North relied on slavery, the more abolitionist sentiment grew because then, the distance from the practice and the recognition that it was unnecessary to prosper created the space to criticize slavery. Abolitionists saw slavery as a human rights issue, whereas the Southerners who still relied on the practice saw it as a property rights issue. The type of slavery that was practiced in America is called chattel slavery. This means that farmers owned humans as their property. So, from their perspective, just like you couldn't just come and claim their cows, in the same way, you could not demand them to release their human slaves because they owned them, much like they owned their animals.

Before the disagreement about slavery, the phenomenon of sectionalism was already in full swing. Although the United States sees itself as one country today, before the Civil War, people acknowledged that they were one nation, but they cleaved to their regional identity more than their national identity. So, someone would be unlikely to describe themselves as an American but would rather introduce themselves as a Northerner or a Southerner. Each group looked at the other as strange or foreign because of their cultural differences. Out of this, sectionalism birthed the debate about states' rights.

Therefore, it is clear that it was not one factor but several moving parts that eventually led to the Civil War. First, the gap in the economies of the North and South produced different perspectives and cultures. This culture bred sectionalism, which evolved into the demand for states' rights. When President Lincoln was elected, the Southerners saw him as an outsider who did not represent them based on their sectionalist attitudes. The industrialization of the North allowed the morality and justice of slavery to be explored, which created the abolitionist sentiment. The factors of economy, slavery, sectionalism, and states' rights were the four intersecting parts that caused the Civil War instead of the simple cause fallacy many promote today.

The "Lost Cause" Myth

Although slavery was not the only reason why the Civil War started, it did play a huge role in initiating the conflict. After the Confederacy lost and slavery was abolished, a new myth was needed to restore the dignity of the Southern States that seceded. Instead of highlighting the integral role of slavery as the fuel that kept the war going, the narrative was reframed to put states' rights at the center of the discourse. In 1866, Edward Pollard published "The Lost Cause: A New Southern History of the War on Confederates" (Ted-ed, 2021). In his writings, Pollard emphasized that states have the right to govern themselves and are only limited by the expressed functions of the national government that were outlined in the Constitution (Ted-ed, 2021). Therefore, according to Pollard, the Confederacy was not fighting to uphold slavery, but it was rather fighting for the right of states to make their own choices.

This myth was promoted and elevated by the United Daughters of the Confederacy (or the UDC), who still exist today. The UDC was established in Nashville, Tennessee, in 1894, and at the height of its popularity, it had over 100,000 members. The UDC raised money to put up monuments of Confederate soldiers in important areas like courthouses. They also got posters of confederates to be put up in public schools. The UDC was instrumental in developing textbooks that downplayed the horrors of slavery and uplifted the Confederate army as heroic defenders of the Constitution. In this way, the pseudohistorical claim of states' rights being the central motivation for the secession of the Southern states was given wind.

The danger of the Lost Cause myth is that it was often used as a bludgeon to slow down racial progress. Whenever movements arose in the United States for the equal treatment of all races, the states' rights argument was reinvigorated as part of the legacy of the Lost Cause. Some promoters of the Lost Cause narrative mention that Confederate leader General Robert E. Lee hated slavery. However, his White supremacist ideals were extensively documented. In the last year of the war, Lee stated that the only valid relationship between White and Black people was that of master and slave.

The issue of Confederate monuments is still contentious today, and the United Daughters of the Confederacy are still working hard to maintain them among other groups. People who cleave to this Lost Cause idea promote the fallacious claim that it is only in recent times that Confederate monuments have become controversial. In 1932, the African American newspaper, The Chicago Defender, conducted a poll asking readers if they would like to see Confederate monuments fall. Almost every respondent was in favor of their abolishment. The readers explained that the abuse they suffered under Jim Crow laws was propped up by the White Southerner reference for these racist Confederate figureheads.

Horrific Chivalry: The Myth of the Genteel South

Southerners valued the idea of being chivalrous. This meant that a gentleman was always expected to act honorably and treat the people around him with respect. He was meant to be kind and polite to women and, in his capacity as a family man, act as an example for people to emulate. However, this chivalrous identity was an incomplete facade. The terrible outcomes of the Civil War, including the suffering of civilians as well as the torturous norms of slavery, showed that Southern chivalry was not as prevalent as many aristocrats pretended it was.

The South's chivalry was questioned after a shocking occurrence on the Senate floor in 1856. Senator Charles Sumner, a staunch abolitionist, gave a speech where he berated Senator Andrew Butler, calling him an idiot while criticizing his commitment to the dehumanizing institution of slavery. The code of chivalry that Southerners in the 1800s embraced required men to defend their families and never allow anybody to dishonor them. The Representative of South Carolina, Preston Brooks, a relative of Sumner, felt that he had to address this discrediting of his state and family. The next day, he assaulted Butler with a gold-tipped cane. Butler never psychologically recovered from the assault and would avoid attending Senate meetings. This highlighted the thin veneer of Southern honor with the brutality hidden just below the surface. The paradox of Southern genteel was now highlighted in a shameful display of violence.

Civilians felt a lack of chivalry on both sides of the war. Innocents were attacked on contested borders and succumbed to the battle's crossfire. About 50,000 civilians were killed during the Civil War, and many lived a life of desperate uncertainty during the conflict. The widespread death filled cemeteries, while injuries overwhelmed hospitals. The reality that there is no such thing as gentlemen in war struck deep into the hearts of the majority of families, all of whom have experienced the loss of loved ones. In the 1800s, there was a high infant mortality rate, but if you made it into the age of being a young adult, it was almost certain you would make it to middle age. What shocked and traumatized many during the Civil War period was that strong young people were meeting untimely deaths.

The Civil War was hell on earth for many Americans, especially for slaves who suffered before and during the war. Slaves had no legal recourse against White people who brutally abused and tortured them under the Southern Slave Codes. Every slave was considered property and would often face dreadful treatment from their slave masters. Slaves were mutilated, whipped, and harshly punished for attempting to run away. Since slaves were property, no consideration was given to their social needs, so families were often separated during sales. Slavery existed all over the world in various forms. Some slaves worked off debt, and in some cultures, slaves had certain rights according to their beliefs.

All slavery was inhumane, but chattel slavery, where a human was equated to a beast, was extremely wicked in its practices. The same aristocracy that prided themselves on their unwritten code of chivalry, which promoted honor and politeness, would inflict unspeakable violence on the people they owned without a sliver of guilt in their conscience. The way that so-called gentlemen of the highest class treated the slaves who produced their wealth is the clearest indication that Southern chivalry was a myth.

The Happy Slave

Abolitionist and former slave Frederick Douglas stood firmly against the myth of the happy slave.
https://commons.wikimedia.org/wiki/File:Frederick_Douglass_(circa_1879).jpg

Abolitionist and former slave Frederick Douglas stood firmly against the myth of the happy slave. In an attempt to downplay the oppression and injustices of slavery, many Southern slave owners crafted the story of the happy slave who sings in the field while working diligently from dusk until dawn. As a former slave, Douglas knew that these descriptions of the happy slave were far from the truth. The subdued attitude that could be misconstrued is a result of the extreme cruelty that slaves experienced. Douglas retold stories of women being stripped down and tied up while whips ripped chucks out of their backs. The hymns that were sung by the religious Christianized Africans were songs of hope and sorrow instead of the joy that deceitful slave masters wanted people to believe.

Some of the religious songs that slaves sang were coded with protest and hope for liberation, making references to Moses, who was the Hebrew liberator, or references to water because the slaves knew that they were brought over from Africa, and they fantasized about returning to the continent for a better life. In addition to the physical trauma that slaves were regularly inflicted with, there was a psychological, social, and cultural disturbance that occurred. Douglas recounts how he felt lost because his master kept him ignorant of his origins.

Many of the cultural traditions and languages of slaves were stripped so that they could settle into a more beast-like state, free from the civilization identifiers from the lands they and their ancestors originated from. Slaves in the Americas found unique ways to preserve their cultural traditions through spiritual systems, like Santeria or Voodoo, where the Gods and spirits from their traditions were masked with Christian saints so that they could secretly practice their lost religions. Some Southern regions, like New Orleans, still have a huge Voodoo tradition as a result of their enslaved past.

Understanding the physical brutality inflicted on slaves, including violent mutilations, murders, rapes, and horrific beatings, reveals that the myth of the happy slave is a far-fetched lie. Add to that the destruction of a culture and the separation of families, and it becomes even clearer that the happy slave is an insulting concoction of the racist imagination that believes Africans should feel comfortable under White subjugation. White supremacy frames Black people as inferior, which means that they should be grateful to come under the control of a superior race.

Challenging the Inevitability of the Civil War

The brewing conflict between the agrarian South, whose entire livelihood was linked to the maintenance of slavery, and the industrial North has led many to believe that the Civil War was inevitable. No compromises could be found through diplomacy, so violence was the only option to resolve a conflict. The compromises proposed in diplomatic efforts to prevent war would have had to maintain slavery to some extent; however, these talks were on the table before the war broke out. As the colonies expanded West into new lands, it opened discussions about whether new territories would be run on the agrarian slave-based economies of the South or if they would move forward with Northern industrialization. These Western territories facilitated some of the first diplomatic talks for both sides to be represented in the United States.

The Missouri Compromise was suggested by Senator Henry Clay in 1820. This compromise would abolish slavery North of the parallel $36°30'$ except for the state of Missouri. In the agreement, Maine would be a free state, while Missouri would be a slave state. Ultimately, this proposal was rejected, but it shows that they were trying to find a balance between slavery and freedom to maintain both South and North ideals and way of life.

Following the Mexican-American war, Senator Henry Clay would again try to find a compromise between freedom and slavery. After the Kansas–Nebraska Act of 1854, which established the territories of Kansas and Nebraska, the Compromise of 1820 was rejected. These territories would not be divided into slave or free by geographical boundaries but were rather left to be governed by the popular opinion of those who inhabited the region. This was done so that settlers would quickly move into the area. However, it resulted in people from both persuasions rushing to the region, causing bloody conflicts that would set the stage for the Civil War.

Another opportunity for a diplomatic solution emerged with the seven debates of Abraham Lincoln and Senator Stephen Douglas. The debates were leading up to an election for the Senator of Illinois. Although Lincoln would lose this election, the coverage of the debates and the texts being published would work in his favor. Lincoln's performance in the debates helped gain him the nomination for the Republican presidency. The main topic of these debates was slavery, and both men went into deep discussion about the institution, making cases for each side.

The nail in the coffin of diplomatic solutions was the election of Lincoln, who was a committed abolitionist. His presidency is what propelled the succession of the Southern States. There were multiple discussions, proposals, and debates leading up to this point about where the Civil War could have been avoided. However, with the hindsight of history, the inability to find a resolution was probably for the best because it led to the freeing of slaves. The Civil War laid the foundations for a free and fair America to emerge from the ashes of the conflict. The freeing of slaves did not equate to a just America for Black people, but it was a step in the right direction.

Chapter 7: Trailblazing Women: Stories of Courage and Transformation

The conflict that started the American Civil War boils down to one basic concept that two factions of the population didn't seem to agree on. That concept was that all humans are born equal. This included the basic human right of being treated with respect and the idea that no one has the right to own, humiliate, or exploit another. As the Northern states embraced these ideals and gradually started to correct the course of unjust actions committed by their ancestors against the slaves, the Southern states seemed hell-bent on maintaining the status quo. Thus, the Civil War erupted. The conflict ebbed and flowed to reach almost every American in the Northern continent. Consequently, many unlikely heroes rose to defy the injustice and steer the war toward the righteous path.

The participation of women in medically aiding the soldiers was one of the main reasons females dominate the nursing field to this day.

Those champions left their imprints in aiding the soldiers medically and retrieving vital information at the risk of their own lives. They aided the helpless and defenseless and worked diligently in documenting the history of the jarring events that unfolded and shaped the lives of all in the country. During the war, many women started stepping up to fill up roles previously occupied by men. The stigma linked to being a woman, meaning staying at home and tending to the young, was set aside so they could fill the functional voids the men left behind by going to war.

Clara Barton and Dorothea Dix - Medical Aid

The participation of women in medically aiding the soldiers was one of the main reasons why females dominate the nursing field to this day.

Before the start of the war, medical staff in most of the hospitsals, whether doctors or nurses, mostly consisted of men. However, with the need for soldiers to fight and the spread of disease from the infected injuries the men endured from the fighting, medical aid was short-handed. Many male nurses in the war hospitals were soldiers who had been wounded in the field and asked to help in tending to more injured soldiers. Many women saw it fit to enter the medical field as nurses to support the staff shortage.

Clara Barton (The Angel of the Battlefield)

Clara Barton was born on December the 25th, 1821, in Oxford, Massachusetts, 40 years prior to the start of the Civil War. Her career started when she was only 15 years old, working as a teacher in nearby schools. She then went on to work in the U.S. Patent Office as a copyist in Washington, D.C., as one of the female pioneers to enter the field of the federal government.

Probably affected by the courageous war stories of her father, when the war started in 1861, Barton volunteered as a nurse, aiding Union soldiers in a makeshift camp in Washington. She was among the women waiting at the train station for the wounded to help organize them into groups that were easily manageable and could receive care efficiently. It is important to note that her first nursing experience came when she was only 11 years old. Her brother had fallen from the roof of a barn, and she spent two long years nursing his wounds until he recovered from a serious cranial injury. She went on to care for soldiers in the Battle of Antietam, where she succeeded in extracting a bullet out of one's face. She tirelessly served in Virginia, North Carolina, and Maryland. Barton had some reservations regarding the efforts made to provide the needed supplies to the soldiers in the field. Deciding to take matters into her own hands, she started to gather many supplies from acquaintances in New Jersey and Massachusetts until she had enough to fill up three warehouses.

Then came the tricky part: finding the means to deliver the supplies to those in the field hospitals. Even though she was adamant about taking the supplies to the destinations herself, she was still fearful of how the soldiers would treat her, given that women who entered the soldier's camps didn't have the best reputations. After a thorough consultation and acquiring the right permissions, she set out on her journey to the site of Battle Cedar. The area was a mountain close to Culpeper in Virginia. She arrived in August of 1862 and went down to work, distributing the much-needed aid.

This journey was the start of a pattern that involved collecting aid, visiting field hospitals, and repeating the cycle repeatedly. Later on, she was granted permission to serve as a nurse on the battlefields. She sympathized with the former slaves and started enlisting many of them as nurses and teaching them how to read.

Near the end of the war, the president at the time, Abraham Lincoln, approved her proposal to start a missing soldiers office. She managed to track down around 20,000 Union soldiers who met their demise in captivity and went on to notify their kin. In 1869, she volunteered at the International Red Cross, which resided in Switzerland.

She was enamored by the organization and its meticulous efforts to relieve those in need. By 1877, she had been given the green light to lead a branch of the organization in America, subsequently helping those afflicted with fires, floods, and earthquakes. She gathered donations nationwide in the form of money, food, and supplies, which helped in aiding around 14,000 survivors. For 23 years, she led the agency through typhoid fever, hurricanes, the aftermath of the Spanish war, and tidal waves. In April of 1912, Clara died at the age of 90 from pneumonia.

Dorothea Dix

Dorothea Dix was born in 1802, and in 1861, she was appointed as the Union's superintendent of female nurses during the Civil War. She was, to some, considered Clara Barton's counterpart in the military. Before the start of the war, she treated the mentally ill and worked on improving confinement conditions for 20 years.

Dorothea was known for her consistency in treating both Union and Confederate soldiers and having disagreements with military personnel. Dorothea created a system for volunteering nurses, having them serve for three-month-long assignments during the war. She was in charge of all the female nurses who operated in army hospitals, noting that she received no pay for the entire duration of the war.

She faced a lot of skepticism and prejudice from military commanders for being a female nurse. She was sure to recruit women who were only above 30, had plain features, and dressed modestly in black and brown skirts with no jewelry or loops.

Dorothea was named by some "Dragon Dix" for being firm, steely, and blunt. Nonetheless, with her leadership of around 3,000 nurses, she served in the Union Army, providing aid to the soldiers. Dix cared about the welfare of her charges as well as the soldiers they tended to. She was often able to secure supplies from private channels when the government made it hard to obtain them. Following the war's end, Dorothea returned to her former employment, supporting the mentally ill.

Rose O'Neal Greenhow and Mary Elizabeth Bowser - Spies

With society at the time underestimating women's roles, resolve, and intellectual abilities, it seemed like the best idea was to employ them as scouts and spies.

Rose Greenhow

Greenhow, also known from a young age as the "Wild Rose," gained renowned stature in Washington society for being the wife of a rich and well-known doctor. Her glamorous life didn't last forever, though, as by 1850, her husband and five of her eight children were deceased. As the war erupted, Rose, an avid Confederate loyalist, created her own ring of spies, gathering information from politicians and diplomats and passing it on to the Confederate General, P.G.T. Beauregard, among others, through coded messages. These messages were sometimes carried by her courier, hidden in her hair.

Her input proved quite useful to the general as it helped him gather his forces to win the first battle of Bull Run against the Union. Greenhow was known for being a skilled conversationalist and hostess; however, that didn't stop the head of the federal government, Allan Pinkerton, from growing suspicious of her activities. He worked hard gathering information to prove her guilt and place her under house arrest with her daughter, little Rose. This action did not deter her from finding other means of transferring information to her contacts. Both she and her eight-year-old daughter were transferred to Old Capitol Prison in 1862. Some months after that, she was moved to Baltimore, Maryland, and received a warm welcome from the Confederate army.

After her release, Greenhow was sent by the Confederate President, Jefferson Davis, to Europe to acquire support for his campaign. On her way back, carrying about $2,000 worth of gold, her ship, The Condor, was pursued by a Union gunship near the North Carolina shore. She went against the captain's orders and tried to escape using a row boat, which ended up capsizing, drowning her, along with the gold she was carrying back to the Confederates.

Mary Elizabeth Bowser - A.K.A. Mary Jane Richards

Unlike Rose Greenhow, Mary was a champion of the Union army. Her birth name was Mary Jane Richards, and she was born a slave to the family of Van Lew of Richmond, Virginia. Even though the will of the late John Van Lew entailed that both his wife and daughter had no right to free the house slaves, it's believed that, secretly, they did just that.

All three women advocated for the Union cause and worked diligently to help them.

Their work included providing sustenance, clothing, letters, medicine, and books to the soldiers, specifically those detained in a nearby military prison (Richmond's brutal Libby Prison). They didn't stop there, though... they would convey messages between the Union prisons and commanders in the army and assist in the release and escape of soldiers from captivity.

In 1863, General Benjamin Butler recruited Elizabeth Van Lew as a spy. The Van Lew women relied on a network of Black and White men and women to achieve these goals. One of those women was Bowser, who earned the name when she married a free Black man, William Bowser, in 1861... the year the war started. Mary was living out of town with her husband at the time when Elizabeth convinced her to join her ring of spies supporting the Union cause.

Mary was subjected to some of the most challenging circumstances in her missions. She worked directly in Davis's home, the rebel president. Since she had a photographic memory, she had no trouble repeating the exact information she saw lying around his desk.

It is unknown how Bowser lived her life after the end of the war.

Susan B. Anthony and Elizabeth Cady – Activists

Susan and Elizabeth were two women who found friendship in their shared ideals for women's rights and anti-slavery movements.

https://commons.wikimedia.org/wiki/File:Elizabeth_Cady_Stanton_and_Susan_B._Anthony.tif

Susan and Elizabeth were two women who found friendship in their shared ideals for women's rights and anti-slavery movements. Growing up, Elizabeth Cady kept herself well-read, learned Greek, and immersed herself in her father's office studying law. In return, instead of expressing his pride, her father kept reminding her of how much more value these efforts would mean had she been a boy.

This type of upbringing, where women were marginalized, considered worthless without a husband, and denied any right to property, was the catalyst that drove Cady to women's rights activism.

As for Susan B. Anthony, she was born in 1820 in Adams, Massachusetts, to a farmer father who went on to become a cotton mill owner and manager and a mother with parents who fought in the American Revolution. From an early age, Susan absorbed her father's ideals that all men were born equal under God. This value continued with her throughout her life, along with her seven brothers and sisters, most of whom advocated for the emancipation of slaves and social justice.

In the spring of 1851, the two women met on the street in Seneca Falls, New York, following the 1st women's rights convention and struck an immediate friendship.

Anthony was described as the strategist of the operation, as she appeared before the congress between 1869 and 1906 to promote women's suffrage. Stanton was more of a writer and an intellectual. She worked hard to bring attention to a lot of women's dilemmas at the time, including birth control and divorce reform, and challenged the ideals that women should have no legal rights in comparison to men.

Together, they founded the American Equal Rights Association and became editors of the association's newspaper, The Revolution, in 1868. The paper was an instrument to spread the ideal that women should have equal rights to men.

During the years of the Civil War, suffragists were advised to put a halt to their fight as slaves had it much worse off than White privileged women. While Anthony agreed with the concept, she made sure to remind people that half of those slaves were also women.

The two women worked hard to gather signatures to pass the 13th Amendment that abolished slavery. In 1870, a rift was created between the two women and other suffragists as the 15th Amendment passed, giving the right to Black men to vote but not women. This was an amendment that they both opposed strongly for the exclusion of the female gender.

In 1872, they registered as voters, along with other women, after they created the Woman Suffrage Association with other activists. As expected, their registration was denied. In November, Anthony voted and then was arrested a few weeks later, found guilty, and charged a fine of 100 dollars. This act awakened national awareness of the women's suffrage movement.

Unfortunately, Anthony passed away 14 years before the 19th Amendment was declared, giving women the right to vote.

Harriet Tubman

Tubman is well known for her efforts in freeing and leading over 300 slaves into safety, including her own parents, operating as a conductor on the Underground Railroad. She was born a slave herself but managed to escape in 1849.

A lot of people have no idea that she also led an elaborate network of spies in South Carolina, mostly made up of former slaves, in favor of the Union officers.

She was the first Black woman to assist and lead a military expedition with Colonel James Montgomery to help free slaves from the rice plantations on the Combahee River. These expeditions caused the Confederate army to lose supply lines, saving around 700 slaves.

She was able to recruit several Black former slaves to slip behind enemy lines, posing as slaves and servants to gather intelligence for the Union army. Tubman was only paid around $200 for her services during the war, forcing her to work small jobs, like selling pies and beer. When she passed away in 1913, she received a burial with military honors at the Fort Hill Cemetery in Auburn, NY.

Sojourner Truth

In 1797, Sojourner Truth was born a slave under the name Isabella Baumfree, a name she later changed. Her childhood was mostly in New York, owned by Dutch American Colonel Johannes Hardenbergh. Throughout her life, she was bought and sold, beaten, and humiliated like most other slaves. Among the tragedies of her life was that in 1815, when she was forced apart from her lover, a fellow slave named Robert, by his master, and instead, was forced to marry another slave named Thomas, with whom she had five children.

Isabella ran away in 1827 after her master died, failing to honor his promises to free her or abide by the New York anti-slavery law. By 1828, she had moved to NY and started working for a minister. She renamed herself Sojourner Truth after declaring that the spirit had called upon her to speak the truth in 1843.

In 1851, during a women's rights conference, Truth delivered her infamous speech, "Ain't I a Woman?" The speech focused on highlighting the evils of slavery and challenged the ideals of any type of inferiority based on gender or race.

In the 1950s, Truth settled down in Battle Creek, Michigan, along with three of her daughters. During the Civil War, she strongly urged young men to enlist and assist the Union army and made efforts to provide supplies to the Black troops.

After the war ended, she was granted the honor of an invitation to the White House.

She got involved in providing freed slaves with paid labor and helping them rebuild their lives with the Freedmen's Bureau. In the late 1860s, she secured several thousand signatures to grant former slaves land. However, her initiative was overlooked, and Congress never implemented it. Her words still ring true to this day, even after her death: "Children, who made your skin white? Was it not God? Who made mine black? Was it not the same God? Am I to blame, therefore, because my skin is black? .... Does not God love colored children as well as white children? And did not the same Savior die to save the one as well as the other?"

Louisa May Alcott and Harriet Beecher Stowe - Writers

One of the most important roles to be played in history is to document it accurately by using words to transcribe and pass the knowledge of what happened in the past so that future generations can learn from it. These two writers did so in the most elegant, entertaining, and creative way possible, and their works of art are still being enjoyed by millions today.

Louisa May Alcott

Louisa focused on introducing readers to strong female characters while simultaneously documenting the harrowing implications of war on families.

https://commons.wikimedia.org/wiki/File:Louisa_May_Alcott,_c._1870_-_Warren%27s_Portraits,_Boston.jpg

---

Louisa was born in 1832 in Philadelphia, Pennsylvania. Her writing focused on introducing readers to strong female characters while simultaneously documenting the harrowing implications of war on families. Young Alcott was inspired by her parents' Transcendentalist movement. Her father was a keen believer that children should enjoy the journey of learning. Her infamous novel, Little Women, mirrored many aspects of her life. Like the heroine of her story, she was one of four sisters: Anna, Abby May, and Elizabeth. Her family was not financially stable, forcing young Alcott to take on jobs, such as teaching and washing laundry, to help out. She turned to writing to try to support her family and herself financially and emotionally.

During the Civil War, in 1861, Louisa served as a nurse in one of the Union hospitals.

While operating as a nurse, she contracted typhoid fever, and her experiences as a patient and as a caretaker inspired her work, _Hospital Sketches_.

She went on to publish her other earlier works under the pen name A.M. Bernard. Later on, one of her publishers asked her to write a novel depicting the life of young women. She drew inspiration from her own childhood with her sisters, and thus, Little Women was born. Not many are aware that later on, she published a story by the name of Little Men after moving to Europe with her sister, May. She was an advocate of the Woman Suffrage Movement and made several publications promoting women's rights. Having no children of her own, when her sister passed away, she adopted her niece. Alcott died in 1888 at the age of 56 in Boston, Massachusetts, after suffering from periods of illnesses throughout her life that she believed stemmed from her service as a nurse and also, possibly contracting mercury poisoning.

Harriet Beecher Stowe

Stowe was born in 1811 in Litchfield, Connecticut. Her father was the congregational minister, Lyman Beecher. Her mother died when she was at the young age of five, and even though her father remarried, she was mostly influenced by her older sister, Catherine, who was 11 years older than her.

She started her education at age eight at the Litchfield Female Academy. She later went on to attend Catherine Beecher's Hartford Female Seminary, which was a program that exposed women to the same courses men were allowed to attend. Stowe showed great writing talent, which was evident in her essays at school. After finishing school, she worked as a teacher for three years (from 1829 to 1832) at the Hartford Female Seminary.

Stowe was exposed to some of the greatest minds of the age when she traveled with her father to Cincinnati, Ohio, following his acceptance to fill the position of president of the esteemed Lane Seminary in 1832. Influenced by the reformers and abolitionists she met, along with the environment in the West, she went on to write her very first book, Primary Geography, in 1833.

Harriet then met her soon-to-be husband, Calvin Stowe, who encouraged her writing. Stowe went on to describe him as "rich in Greek & Hebrew, Latin & Arabic, & alas! rich in nothing else...".

She bore seven children with him, six of whom were born in Cincinnati. In 1849, she had the misfortune of experiencing something that every parent dreads and fears. Her son, Samuel Charles Stowe, who was only 18 months old, died of cholera. The pain she experienced from this loss inspired her story, Uncle Tom's Cabin. The story allowed her a deeper understanding of what slave women suffered through when their children were stolen and sold to the highest bidder.

In 1950, following the passage of the Fugitive Slave Act, Harriet took to writing stories about the horrors that slavery inflicted on human beings. One of her sources for her stories was a slave called John Andrew Jackson, who took refuge in her and her husband's home on his escape route to Canada.

Near the beginning of the Civil War, in 1862, she traveled to the capital, Washington D.C., and met with President Lincoln. It is unclear what the exact conversation that went on between them was about, though some people stated that the president credited her with writing the book that started the war.

After the war ended, she moved to Jacksonville, Florida, and worked as an editor for a magazine called Hearth and Home. In 1888, it was said that the author was afflicted with Alzheimer's, and she rewrote her famous book, Uncle Tom's Cabin, believing it was a new piece of artwork. She died at her home in Connecticut in 1896. In her obituary, it stated that she died from a year-long mental trouble that caused congestion in the brain and partial paralysis.

Chapter 8: Survival Stories of the Civil War

The Civil War was one of the deadliest periods in American history. In terms of the percentage of the population that died, this war is one of the most brutal wars ever recorded in modern times. Many soldiers were captured during prolonged battles and were placed into prison camps. Overcrowding, dilapidated shelters, lack of food, and poor sanitation resulted in many prisoners getting sick and dying. Both the Union and Confederate armies were not able to cope with the flood of prisoners that kept pouring in. Therefore, civil society had to step up and provide the support that was needed. Individuals and organizations provide resources sometimes at great detriment to themselves. These off-battlefield heroes are often forgotten when glory is passed around for the courageous accompaniments of people in the war.

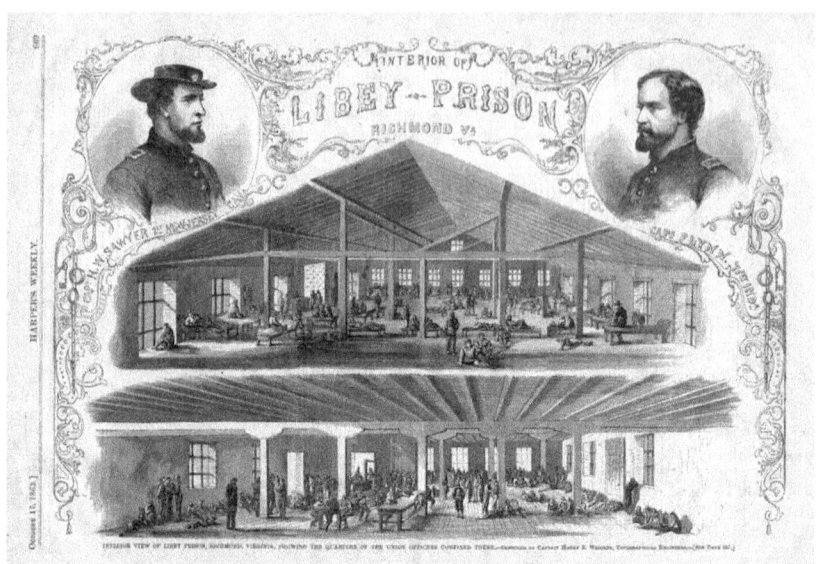

The prisons were typically makeshift sites made from repurposed buildings or wood if you were lucky.

https://commons.wikimedia.org/wiki/File:Libby_Prison_interior.jpg

In addition to the prison camps, especially in those that led up to the war, slaves were still held in similarly horrific conditions. Organizations, like churches, as well as individuals who promoted the abolishment of slavery, came together to assist slaves who escaped so that they could get to the North. The humanity that was shown to dehumanize slaves and enemy combatants in one of the bloodiest times highlights the paradox of war and oppression because, out of these conditions, heartwarming acts of kindness flourished.

Captives during the Civil War

During the bloody battles of the Civil War, many soldiers were captured. After surrendering or being subdued, soldiers would get taken into custody. Soldiers who tried to flee and were caught also suffered the fate of being imprisoned. Civilians were imprisoned for providing information to enemy soldiers. The conditions in Civil War prison camps were horrendous. The prisons were typically makeshift sites made from repurposed buildings or wood if you were lucky. Most of the time, the prisons were canvas tents that were constructed by the prisoners themselves. The sanitation standards were non-existent, and food was scarce because resources had to be stretched to support the fighting men.

Poor sanitation, coupled with the lack of nutrition, resulted in widespread malnutrition and the rampant spread of diseases. Furthermore, medical science had yet to advance in many areas. Surgery was crude, and there was no understanding of germs, so infections were common, causing death or the loss of limbs. The modern pharmaceutical field was still in its infancy, and some medicines were experimental. 400,000 soldiers were imprisoned, and around 56,000 died. That is more than double the percentage of prisoners that die in federal prisons today.

The mental health of prisoners kept in these inhumane conditions deteriorated rapidly. The psychological field barely existed in this period, but by the description of survivors, it is reasonable to conclude that in addition to PTSD, which is a common outcome of war, prisoners developed psychosis and schizophrenia. Prisoners were packed like matchsticks, so diseases like mumps and smallpox spread rapidly. The unsanitary state of the prison also fueled cases of dysentery, diarrhea, and typhoid fever. Primitive and uniform treatments, like bleeding or medicine containing arsenic, only served to worsen the health conditions of prisoners. Most of the time, prisoners were left for dead as medical resources had to be reserved for soldiers.

The country was actively at war, so the prisoners were treated with extreme disdain. Beatings were common, and no regard was given to their humanity. Their cramped cells, limited food, and nowhere to bathe left prisoners filthy, sick, and weak. When prisoners were released, their pale, leathery skin gripped their frail bodies so tightly that it exposed every bone. If a sick prisoner entered the camp, it was a death sentence for huge groups of people whose immune systems were weakened by malnutrition and the conditions they were held captive in.

Confederate Prisons: Andersonville and Libby Prison

Andersonville prison, in Georgia, is where the Confederate army held their captives. This prison was one of the worst examples of the inhumane treatment of prisoners. Captain Henry Wirz, who ran the prison, was executed for war crimes because of how poor the conditions at Andersonville were. He was accused of not providing shelter and food for the prisoners as a method of torturous neglect. However, through modern eyes, he is not painted with such a wicked color. The conditions at the prison may have been due to a lack of supplies, so the captain had no option but to run the prison in such a cruel way. The argument about Wirz and whether he deliberately neglected the prisoners or if it was a result of food shortages in the Confederate states is still ongoing among historians. At its worst, the prison held eight times more people than it was meant to.

Prisoners survived on corn meal and bacon. There were no fruits or vegetables in the rations, which caused scurvy due to the lack of vitamin C. One of the worst sanitary nightmares at Andersonville prison was that excrement was mixed with the drinking water because prisoners relived themselves close to the water source. A prisoner writes about how every morning, when he'd look for friends and acquaintances, he would pass by at least a dozen corpses. Although Andersonville is highlighted as an infamously deadly prison, these conditions were common in many prison camps on both sides.

Libby prison, which was similarly notorious, was constructed in the heart of Confederate territory in Richmond, Virginia. The building had many businesses, including a grocery store, a shipping plant, and a tobacco factory, before it was converted into a wartime prison. Libby was unique because it was for officers only, and it was used as a base for processing. Prisoners were shoved into the three-story building from wall to wall, with no furniture, so they felt the bite of the environment. Libby prison was used as a propaganda punching bag as the media published stories of food shortages and diseases being common at the prison. Escapes and rescue attempts have grown the legend of Libby in popular imagination. To assist in the care of captives on their side, the Union sent supplies to Libby, but they had to stop because the food was being used to feed the Confederate army.

Union Prisons: Elmira and Camp Douglas

Unlivable conditions in prisons were not unique to the Confederacy. Elmira was, by far, one of the most inhumane camps in the Northern territories. Elmira only functioned as a prison camp for about a year. Before it held Confederate captives, the prison site was a recruitment depot where soldiers who were newly enlisted went for basic training. Later on, it became a draft rendezvous point, eventually evolving into a prison camp in 1865.

The camp held over 12,000 prisoners of war when it was built to hold just 5,000. This meant that they were at more than double the capacity that the prison was constructed for, which brought along with it a mountain of issues. The barracks were not enough to hold all the imprisoned soldiers, so tent cities were erected along the Chemung River. Almost 3,000 prisoners died due to the extreme weather of the North, along with unsanitary conditions and lack of food and medicine. Ailments like dysentery, smallpox, and pneumonia were commonplace, with no doctors to care for the dying men. Today, the human rights abuses that took place at Elmira are noted, but the plight of the prisoners was swept under the rug as rumors for 130 years. The end of the war – where the South was declared the bad guys and the North the victors – meant that the suffering of Confederate soldiers was justified. The mounting evidence and stories of abuse eventually led to mainstream figureheads and the general population admitting that the horrific treatment of prisoners occurred on the site.

Camp Douglas, much like Elmira, began as a training camp in 1861, but by 1862, it had become a place to imprison Confederate rebels. Like many of the prisons of the Civil War era, health and safety were not major concerns. Camp Douglas's weak security resulted in many of the inmates escaping. One in seven prisoners died in this Chicago prison. A mass liberation from the prison was planned but was stopped with the help of informants. 4,000 people met the end in the foul conditions of the prison. A U.S. Sanitary Commission agent described how the smell of excrement hung heavy in the air as it seeped into the soil of the land (Karamanski, 2005). He continued to describe how the conditions were unbearable and how it instilled within him great despair.

Civilians, Women, and Children in Prisons

It was rare that civilians were imprisoned in one of the 150 prison camps that were operational in the Civil War unless they directly assisted military personnel on either side. The predominant population of the prisoners was soldiers captured during battles. Women would get captured when they acted as spies, informing them of the comings and goings of the groups they considered their enemies. Women could not hold political offices at the time due to discrimination, but they did have a political consciousness that drove their decision-making about which side they would support and how they could assist them through messaging and action.

Women played a powerful role in the Civil War period by taking care of the homes as their men were sent out into the disease-ridden camps to lay their lives on the line for what they believed in. Women took over the roles that the men had previously held, like farmers, workers, and business owners. Some of them were nurses who treated those injured in battle. These gender roles defined much of the war, but there were still women who creatively found their way onto battlefields, which risked them getting captured and being placed into prison camps.

Women were not allowed to join the military on either side of the Civil War, but some felt compelled to stand and fight for their ideals either out of their political and cultural will or to seek vengeance for the husbands and children they had lost. To bear arms, women would disguise themselves as men so that they could end up on the frontlines. They bravely fought, just like their male counterparts, and took their prison time just as the men did. Some women remained hidden in their secret identities until they were either captured or killed. Some estimates say that there were at least 400 women soldiers during the Civil War.

Many children ended up in prison camps because child soldiers were, unfortunately, a common occurrence during the war. The Confederacy had no minimum age for boys to join, with some as young as 10 ending up in the heat of battle. The Union placed their minimum age of enlistment at 18, but this was often overlooked, with child soldiers joining their side as well. About 20% of the soldiers who fought in the Civil War were under the age of 18, which meant that a significant chunk of prisoners housed in horrendous conditions were teenage children.

Escape Stories

Arguably, the most legendary escape from a Civil War prison camp was at Libby. The overcrowded conditions meant that guards weren't able to patrol and secure every inmate effectively. This allowed prisoners to plot, scheme, and devise an elaborate escape. In February 1864, over 100 prisoners tunneled out of the camp. 59 of them made it back to friendly Union territory. The escape gave the Union soldiers undue confidence, so they attempted a rescue a few weeks later. The rescue was led by General H. Judson Kilpatrick and Colonel Ulric Dahlgren. The failed liberation attempt cost many Union soldiers their lives and prompted the strengthening of security measures in the prison. The Libby officers dug tunnels and filled them with mines to prevent any rescues or escapes in the future.

A failed rescue which was led by General H. Judson Kilpatrick and Colonel Ulric Dahlgren took place.

Fort Delaware was a Union-run prison that held Confederate soldiers and prominent political prisoners. The prison was established in 1862, and the conditions were bearable by the standards of the time. As the war progressed, an influx of prisoners was transported to the fort, resulting in the typical unhealthy and overcrowded conditions of Civil War prisons. The hot and humid summers and cold winters caused many prisoners to develop illnesses and die. Furthermore, there was an epidemic of lice and bedbugs that caused infections in the prison. Escapees risked their lives to swim across the freezing Delaware River, with not many of them making it to their intended destination. The 3,000 guards to 12,000 prisoners resulted in many attempted escapes, with some estimates going into the thousands.

Andersonville is the most notorious of all the Civil War prisons because it is the most well-known. Despite being so popular, the conditions at the prison were a norm at the time and were only highlighted and singled out for propaganda purposes. Around 351 prisoners escaped from Andersonville, which was just under 1% of the total population. Many of the escapees were recaptured and returned to prison, which meant that the inmates who found freedom were even fewer. The tiny amount of one in 1,400 prisoners escaping was recorded at the brutal Andersonville prison camp. Some soldiers who escaped never returned to the battlefield but quietly disappeared into a life of obscurity in order to avoid the merciless frontlines, and opting to spend the rest of their time on Earth with their families.

The Underground Railroad

The abolitionist movement slowly gained steam, eventually culminating in all-out war. The anti-slave sentiment started among religious groups, like the Quakers, whom George Washington accused of attempting to free his slaves in 1786, decades before the Civil War. In the 1800s, the abolition of slavery began picking up steam with the African Methodist Episcopal Church, which was established in 1816, joining the fight against slavery and helping slaves escape. These were the early iterations of what would become known as the Underground Railroad.

The Underground Railroad is not what the name suggests. There were no tracks carrying slaves to freedom. The railroad was a network of people and organizations that helped slaves escape to the free North in the lead-up to the Civil War. The Underground Railroad assisted slaves from the states that bordered regions with abolitionist sentiments, like Kentucky, Maryland, and Virginia. People who harbored these fugitives on their way to freedom were known as conductors. These conductors would hide runaway slaves in homes, churches, and schools run by individuals identified as stationmasters.

One of the most prominent conductors was the escaped slave Harriet Tubman. Tubman escaped a plantation in Maryland along with her brothers. She returned multiple times, inspired by a vision from God to free the slaves. She helped many who escaped get into Canada because she believed that in the United States, they would still be treated horribly. Another big name in the railroad industry was the famous writer and former slave Frederick Douglas. He dedicated his life to the liberation of Black people even after the end of the war. Douglas helped over 400 escaped slaves make their way into Canada from his home in Rochester, New York. William Still, whose parents had escaped slavery, worked closely with Tubman. The records that he kept are how many of the stories of the Underground Railroad have been transmitted through the generations. Many individuals who were inspired by religion, politics, and ideologies stood against slavery and acted upon their beliefs of helping slaves escape at great risk to themselves. Without the connections of the Underground Railroad, many slaves might have never gotten to taste freedom.

Support for Captives

Being kept as a prisoner in the Civil War skyrocketed your chances of dying. The support that was provided by civil groups and families is what kept many people alive through the traumatizing experience. One of these amazing people was nurse Phoebe Yates Pember, of Chimborazo Hospital. Pember treated both Confederate and Union soldiers in Virginia, which was one of the most violent states at the time, located in the heart of the Confederate country. Supplies were constantly low, and food shortages ravaged entire communities. Pember fought the losing battle of making do with what she had while she was also starving. Medical staff at the hospital would neglect to feed themselves so that patients and prisoners could eat. This selflessness is a symbol of how people can draw closer together during difficult times.

Kate Cumming, a Confederate nurse, provided captives at the infamous Andersonville prison with supplies like clothing and material to build a kitchen. Despite her disdain for Union soldiers, she still assisted them, most likely because her humanity would not allow her to ignore their situation. Other nurses, like Ada W. Bacot, also remarked about the pity she felt for the Union soldiers despite her political affiliations. As much as political indoctrination can cause people to take some of the most evil actions against fellow people, the empathy that is evolutionarily ingrained can rise to the top so much that you would go out of your way to care for the enemy. These kinds of women put their political beliefs aside so that they could help those they were meant to hate. No matter what people get indoctrinated with, it is unnatural to take pleasure in seeing people suffer.

Civilian organizations, like the United States Sanitary Commission, also did their part to assist the wounded and ill who were imprisoned. The organization would fundraise and gain donations so that they could distribute supplies like clothing and medicine around the country. The United States Sanitary Commission did not take any funds from the government... they were completely supported by the people on the ground. In addition to distributing essential supplies, like food, they also provided education on how to treat sick or injured prisoners properly. Other relief organizations, like the Women's Central Association of Relief, worked under the United States Sanitary Commission, while others, like the U.S. Christian Commission, functioned more independently, doing the same kind of life-saving work in the harshest conditions. These organizations helped people on both sides.

Chapter 9: Reconciliation in the Post-War Years: Stories of Healing and Unity

The thunderous echoes of cannon fire had faded, and the once-battle-scarred landscapes were now draped in a tentative calm. The Civil War had ended, leaving in its wake a nation grappling with the haunting aftermath of a conflict that had pitted brother against brother. As weary and weathered soldiers began their journey home, the United States faced a new challenge: rebuilding not only its fractured cities but also the shattered bonds of its people.

The challenge lay not only in reconstructing physical structures but also in rebuilding the intangible bonds of a nation seeking solace and unity.

This chapter will help you look into the compelling stories of those who returned from the frontlines — soldiers who had donned blue and gray uniforms, fighting for causes that had torn the nation asunder. Their experiences, both triumphant and tragic, are windows into a tumultuous era when healing and unity became paramount.

Picture a Union soldier, battle-worn and emotionally scarred, finally reuniting with family after years of separation. The joy and relief, tinged with the profound changes wrought by the war, create a poignant tableau of the human cost of conflict. On the other side, envision a Confederate soldier navigating the delicate path of rebuilding relationships strained by ideology and bloodshed. Communities, once divided along ideological lines, now faced the formidable task of rediscovering common ground.

This chapter embarks on a journey through the landscapes of post-war America, where stories of resilience, reconciliation, and renewal emerge like sprouts breaking through scorched earth. It explores not only the individual struggles of soldiers readjusting to civilian life but also the collective efforts of communities striving to mend the fabric of a nation torn apart.

The emotional toll of the war's aftermath was something that could not be overlooked. The challenge lay not only in reconstructing physical structures but also in rebuilding the intangible bonds of a nation seeking solace and unity.

Reconnecting with Family and Loved Ones

As the dust settled on the battlefields, soldiers from both the Union and the Confederacy faced the arduous journey of returning to civilian life. Their experiences ranged from the jubilant reunions of Union soldiers with their families to the challenging process of rebuilding relationships for Confederate veterans.

Emotional Reunions

Imagine the scene as Union soldiers, clad in worn uniforms and bearing the physical and emotional scars of war, finally returned to their hometowns. Families, long separated by the cruel exigencies of conflict, embraced their returning heroes with tears of joy. Soldiers who had endured the brutality of battle now sought solace in the familiar arms of loved ones. These reunions, while heartwarming, were also marked by the palpable changes wrought by the war, with some soldiers grappling with the lingering trauma of the battlefield.

One poignant example is the account of Private John Thompson, who, after surviving the Battle of Gettysburg, returned to his family in Ohio. The emotional weight of the war was etched across his face as he reunited with a wife who had endured years of uncertainty. Beneath the surface of joy lingered the shadows of trauma. Private Thompson, like countless others, carried the weight of the battlefield in his heart. The sounds of cannons, the faces of fallen comrades, and the specter of war haunted his every step. His struggle to reintegrate into the rhythm of civilian life mirrored the broader challenge faced by a nation attempting to reconcile with its own scars.

Challenges of Readjustment

The return to civilian life presented its own set of challenges for Union veterans. Many struggled with physical disabilities, haunted by the echoes of war that reverberated in their minds. Unemployment and economic hardships compounded the difficulties, forcing veterans to navigate a landscape forever altered by the conflict.

A vivid illustration of this struggle is found in the letters of Sergeant James Miller, who, after sustaining injuries in battle, faced the daunting task of finding employment to support his family. His poignant words reflect the common thread of hardship running through the lives of many Union veterans.

In one letter, Miller writes of the challenges he faced in securing a job suitable for a man who had borne the weight of a nation's strife. The scars on his body, once badges of honor, now posed barriers to reintegration into the workforce. The echoes of war that reverberated in his mind manifested not only in physical limitations but also in the psychological hurdles of readjusting to a society that had moved forward, often forgetting the sacrifices of its warriors.

Unemployment and economic hardships compounded the difficulties faced by Union veterans. The war had disrupted industries, and the post-war period was marked by a landscape in flux. Jobs were scarce, and economic stability remained elusive for many who had returned with dreams of rebuilding their lives. The economic fallout of war created a formidable barrier to the smooth reintegration of veterans into civilian life.

Efforts to Rebuild Relationships

On the Confederate side, soldiers returned to a South ravaged by war, where the task of rebuilding extended beyond physical structures to the very fabric of society. Families torn apart by ideological differences sought reconciliation, with returning soldiers attempting to mend the fractures caused by their choices.

The story of Captain Robert Anderson serves as a compelling example. A Confederate officer, he faced the challenge of rebuilding his relationship with a brother who had fought on the side of the Union. Their journey toward reconciliation reflects the broader efforts of families to bridge the chasm created by the Civil War.

The process of reconciliation required a delicate balance of understanding and forgiveness. Families engaged in difficult conversations, acknowledging the complexities that had led to their divisions. The wounds inflicted by the war were not only physical but also psychological, and healing necessitated a mutual recognition of the toll exacted on all sides.

This effort to rebuild relationships was not limited to individual families; it extended to communities grappling with the aftermath of the war. Churches, often at the center of Southern communities, became crucial spaces for collective healing. Congregations, once divided along ideological lines, sought common ground and shared values to bridge the gaps created by the conflict.

Communities Coming Together

In towns and cities across the Confederacy, communities faced the dual challenge of healing internal divisions and rebuilding the foundations of society. Churches, once divided by loyalties, became spaces for collective healing and unity. Community-driven initiatives that aimed at supporting returning veterans, both materially and emotionally, played a crucial role in the reconstruction of Southern life.

An emblematic story is that of the small town of Appomattox, where, despite their Confederate sympathies, residents extended a hand of friendship to returning Union soldiers. This microcosm of unity reflected the broader Southern sentiment of rebuilding as a united community.

Forgiveness and Understanding

Amid the remnants of a nation scarred by civil strife, individual stories of forgiveness and understanding emerged as beacons of hope. In the aftermath of the Civil War, former enemies on both sides of the conflict grappled with the profound task of reconciliation, showcasing the power of forgiveness in healing wounds and fostering unity.

Former Enemies Reconciling

The war had sewn deep divisions, pitting brother against brother and friend against friend. Yet, amid the rubble of animosity, stories of former enemies reconciling emerged. These narratives often transcended the boundaries of the battlefield, unfolding in the intimate spaces of homes and communities.

Consider the tale of Sarah and Emily, childhood friends from Georgia whose loyalties diverged during the war — Sarah supporting the Union cause while Emily siding with the Confederacy. Post-war, they faced the challenge of reconciling their differences and rebuilding their friendship. Their journey serves as a microcosm of a nation attempting to knit together the torn fabric of unity.

Friendships Across Battle Lines

The power of forgiveness manifested in unexpected friendships that blossomed across battle lines. Soldiers who had once squared off on opposite ends of the battlefield found common ground, transcending the scars of war to form enduring connections.

The friendship between Union soldier Thomas and Confederate soldier William is illustrative. Captured during the same skirmish, their shared experiences as prisoners of war forged a bond that endured beyond the conflict. Their story reflects the human capacity for understanding and camaraderie, even in the face of bitter enmity.

Communities Fostering Understanding

Beyond individual narratives, entire communities embarked on a collective journey toward forgiveness and understanding. Churches, often central to the fabric of American communities, played a pivotal role in fostering reconciliation. Sermons and communal gatherings became spaces for reflection, dialogue, and, ultimately, healing.

A notable example is a Southern church congregation that extended an invitation to a Union chaplain to address their community. The chaplain's message of reconciliation resonated, becoming a catalyst for renewed connections and understanding among former adversaries.

Empathy's Role in Post-War Unity

Empathy emerged as a cornerstone in the quest for post-war unity. Individuals, whether Union or Confederate sympathizers, began to empathize with the suffering and struggles of their fellow countrymen. This shared understanding became a potent force in mending the torn social fabric.

Mary Johnson, a widow from a Confederate family, opened her home to Union war orphans, demonstrating a remarkable act of empathy. Her decision (met with initial skepticism) ultimately became a symbol of reconciliation as the children found a new family and a home where wounds could heal.

In the intricate dance of forgiveness and understanding, the post-war years bore witness to a nation grappling with the complexities of healing. These individual and communal stories of reconciliation laid the groundwork for a broader exploration of the societal mechanisms that aimed to bind the wounds of a fractured America.

Presidential Pardons and Reconciliation Policies

The post-war period brought with it the weighty task of reconciling a nation torn apart by civil conflict. Presidential pardons, epitomized by Abraham Lincoln's magnanimous vision of "Malice toward none, with charity for all," played a crucial role in shaping the trajectory of reconciliation. Additionally, amnesties and oaths of allegiance emerged as tools to restore citizenship rights and mend the frayed fabric of American society.

"Malice Toward None, with Charity for All"

Abraham Lincoln's second inaugural address, delivered in the waning days of the war, outlined a vision for post-war reconciliation. His words echoed a sentiment of magnanimity, calling for unity and forgiveness. The famous phrase, "Malice toward none, with charity for all," encapsulated Lincoln's aspiration for a nation that could move beyond the bitterness of war.

Lincoln's approach was not merely rhetorical. He implemented policies aimed at rebuilding the nation rather than perpetuating animosity. The Proclamation of Amnesty and Reconstruction outlined conditions for Southern states to rejoin the Union, emphasizing a lenient and inclusive path to reconciliation.

Impact on Post-War Policies

Lincoln's vision influenced subsequent policies and shaped the Reconstruction era. His commitment to a swift and inclusive restoration of the Southern states aimed to expedite the healing process. However,

Lincoln's tragic assassination in 1865 left the nation grappling with the challenge of implementing his vision without his direct leadership.

Tools for Restoring Citizenship Rights

Post-war reconciliation required mechanisms to restore citizenship rights to those who had sided with the Confederacy. Amnesties, often granted through proclamations, provided a blanket pardon to individuals, allowing them to regain their civil rights. These measures aimed to facilitate a comprehensive healing process.

An illustrative case is the Amnesty Proclamation of 1868, which extended a full pardon to most former Confederates, enabling their reintegration into the political and social fabric of the nation. This blanket amnesty marked a significant step in moving toward a united and inclusive America.

Role in Rebuilding the Nation

Oaths of allegiance became another instrument in the process of rebuilding. Individuals seeking pardon were required to swear allegiance to the Union, symbolizing a commitment to the restored nation. While these oaths varied in stringency, they collectively contributed to the broader goal of reuniting the nation under a shared allegiance.

The story of a Confederate veteran, James Monroe, exemplifies this process. After taking the oath of allegiance, Monroe became an active participant in Reconstruction efforts, embodying the transformative power of reconciliation policies.

Challenges to Reconciliation

While the post-war years witnessed earnest attempts at reconciliation, the journey toward unity was fraught with challenges. The rise of the Ku Klux Klan, resistance to reconstruction efforts, and the ongoing struggles for civil rights and social justice all cast shadows on the nation's path to healing.

The Rise of the Ku Klux Klan

**U. S. KLANS
KNIGHTS OF THE KU-KLUX-KLAN,**
INCORPORATED

Yesterday, Today

We Are Not

A Hate

Organization

Equal

But

Separate

Rights

**and Forever
THE KLAN RIDES AGAIN**

The Ku Klux Klan (KKK) emerged as a dark force, opposing the efforts of reconciliation and fostering an atmosphere of intimidation and violence.
Ku Klux Klan, CC0, via Wikimedia Commons:
https://commons.wikimedia.org/wiki/File:Flier_advertising_the_Ku_Klux_Klan_(KKK).jpg

The Ku Klux Klan (KKK) emerged as a dark force, opposing the efforts of reconciliation and fostering an atmosphere of intimidation and violence. Comprising of mostly Confederate veterans, this clandestine organization sought to undermine the newfound civil rights of freed slaves and impede the progress made during the Reconstruction era.

The Klan's tactics, including acts of terrorism, targeted both African Americans and sympathetic Whites, creating an atmosphere of fear that hindered the nation's journey toward true reconciliation.

Challenges to Reconstruction

The KKK's activities posed a direct challenge to the Reconstruction efforts aimed at integrating the Southern states back into the Union. Its violent tactics, such as lynching and intimidation, sought to reverse the social and political advancements made during this period.

In response, the federal government implemented measures to suppress Klan activities, including the Enforcement Acts of 1870 and

1871. However, the KKK's influence persisted, leaving a lasting impact on the struggle for civil rights.

Ongoing Struggles for Civil Rights

The end of the Civil War marked the formal abolition of slavery, a monumental step towards equality. However, the promise of civil rights for African Americans faced formidable challenges. The Reconstruction Amendments — the 13th, 14th, and 15th — were enacted to secure rights for the newly freed population. Despite these amendments, the battle for civil rights continued.

Despite gaining the right to vote, African Americans faced widespread disenfranchisement through discriminatory laws, such as poll taxes and literacy tests. These obstacles undermined the vision of true equality and hampered the nation's progress toward reconciliation.

Shaping the Trajectory of Social Justice

The struggles for civil rights in the post-war years laid the foundation for the broader social justice movements of the 20th century. The seeds planted during Reconstruction blossomed into the Civil Rights Movement, which aimed to dismantle segregation and systemic racism.

Visionaries like Frederick Douglass and leaders of the burgeoning civil rights movement, such as Martin Luther King Jr., drew inspiration from the unfulfilled promises of post-war reconstruction. Their tireless efforts reshaped the narrative of reconciliation, emphasizing the need for a more just and equitable society.

As the nation confronted the challenges posed by the Ku Klux Klan, resistance to reconstruction, and the ongoing struggles for civil rights, the path to reconciliation proved to be an intricate and often tumultuous journey. These challenges, both historical and persistent, underscored the complexity of forging true unity in the aftermath of a deeply divisive conflict.

As you reflect on the post-war years, the tapestry of reconciliation, healing, and unity emerges as a complex and multifaceted narrative. The stories of soldiers returning home, individual acts of forgiveness, presidential pardons, and the persistent challenges with reconciliation collectively paint a portrait of a nation grappling with the aftermath of the Civil War.

The return of soldiers to their families, marked by emotional reunions and efforts to rebuild relationships, symbolized the personal toll of the war. Communities, both in the North and South, engaged in collective endeavors to heal and rebuild, emphasizing the resilience of the American spirit. Individual stories of forgiveness and understanding showcased the remarkable capacity of the human spirit to transcend bitterness and forge connections. Friendships that emerged across battle lines and communities fostering empathy became powerful instruments in the broader process of healing societal wounds.

Abraham Lincoln's vision of reconciliation, embodied in his second inaugural address, influenced post-war policies that sought to reintegrate the Southern states. Amnesties and oaths of allegiance became tools for restoring citizenship rights and mending the nation's fractured fabric. The battles fought during the post-war years laid the groundwork for future movements striving for justice and equality.

The struggles for civil rights in the post-war years did not conclude with the Reconstruction era. Instead, they set the stage for the broader civil rights movements of the 20th century, shaping the trajectory of American society and influencing the ongoing pursuit of equality. The post-war period provides valuable lessons about the challenges and triumphs of reconciliation. While significant progress has been made, the echoes of the Civil War persist in contemporary discussions about race, justice, and the ongoing quest for a more complete union.

In conclusion, the post-war years were a crucible of reconciliation, testing the resilience of a nation fractured by civil strife. The stories of individuals, communities, and the overarching efforts to heal and unite offer timeless lessons about the complexities of forging unity in the face of division.

Chapter 10: The Civil War's Enduring Legacy: Modern Perspectives and Contemporary Reflections

This final chapter analyzes how the memory of the Civil War has been preserved and commemorated through monuments, which have often sparked controversies and debates about their removal or reinterpretation. The second narrative examines the link between the Civil War and the modern civil rights movement, highlighting key events in the struggle for racial equality.

The third story explores how the Civil War continues to shape America's national identity. The fourth one examines the influence of Civil War military tactics and innovations on modern warfare. Lastly, the chapter analyzes how the Civil War is portrayed in art and popular culture and the ways it continues to captivate modern audiences.

The first truly significant establishment that commemorated the war was the first National Military Park, built at Chickamauga and Chattanooga in 1890.

Gary Todd from Xinzheng, China, CC0, via Wikimedia Commons:
https://commons.wikimedia.org/wiki/File:Chickamauga_and_Chattanooga_National_Military_Park_(10484039133).jpg

Civil War Monuments and Controversies

Proud of their contribution to the war, Civil War veterans watched in dismay as the battlefield where they fought so hard began to change. By the early 1880s, the population of the towns near the former battles was rapidly expanding, and the veterans were afraid that their battlefields would soon be covered by buildings. While some veterans began to place monuments as early as the war ended, these were small. The first truly significant establishment that commemorated the war was the first National Military Park, built at Chickamauga and Chattanooga in 1890. It was the result of a joint effort between veterans from both sides who wished to offer an accurate tool for studying the Civil War. The park's battlefield simulators are still being utilized by military units from around the world. Besides the park, there are thousands of small markers and monuments to commemorate where battles unfolded, what decisions led to them, and why, and offering a lesson from the past that can be used in the future. These are placed near (not always accurately denoting the battle's exact place) the battlefields of Antietam, Chickamauga-Chattanooga, Vicksburg, Gettysburg, and Shiloh. A vast majority of these honor entire Civil War units rather than commemorating individuals.

The first monument was placed by Union veterans, who bought small plots of land from locals and employed a manufacturer to design and build a piece memorializing the deeds of their unit and the actions of their fallen comrades. Before joining forces to build parks, Union veterans founded the building of all monuments on their own.

Confederate monuments took a while to rise, and they only started in 1900. After the war, the Southern economy lay in shambles. The only ones who could pay for the monuments were widows and daughters of former Confederate soldiers. They even had to raise the funds by holding tea parties and selling their books. The majority of the pieces were placed by 1918, and a few after, during the Civil War Centennial period concluding in 1965.

Besides indicating the approximate position of military units during battles, some monuments are also dedicated to the courageous actions and tremendous sacrifice of men and women, like the Clara Barton monument at Antietam, the stand at Chickamauga's Horseshoe Ridge, and the station near the Wheatfield at Gettysburg. Even nowadays, these serve as places for quiet remembrance. However, during the subsequent wars, some of the larger monuments were used as training grounds by the United States Army. For example, the Camp Colt marker at Gettysburg was used as a training field for a unit led by Captain Dwight D. Eisenhower during World War I.

Creators of the individual monuments aimed to preserve their symbolism while utilizing the artistic traditions at the time they were created. Some of the artists behind the most prominent Civil War monuments are Augustus Saint-Gaudens, Gutzon Borglum, and Felix de Weldon. James Kelly is another artist who created Civil War monuments and had a rather unique approach to meeting or looking up the subject of his art or meeting with his comrades if the work was dedicated to a fallen individual. He is best known for sculpting the statue of General John Buford, which is now placed at Gettysburg.

Other Civil War monuments include the national cemeteries at Shiloh, Antietam, Gettysburg, Fredericksburg, Chattanooga, and other significant battlefields. Here, on these protected grounds, lie the bodies and/or memories of fallen men and women who contributed to their causes with their heroic deeds. Additional small statues and tablets were placed among the war heroes' headstones. A great example of this is found in the Minnesota section of Soldiers National Cemetery, where a stone memorial commemorates the brave actions of the 1st Minnesota Infantry. Fredericksburg National Cemetery hosts monuments to the Confederate units, including Parker's Battery, which excelled in the Second Battle of Fredericksburg. Shiloh National Cemetery, which was once an integral part of the Union defensive line, has a monument dedicated to the 9th Illinois Infantry.

As magnificent as they are, the Civil War monuments have sparked numerous controversies over the years. This primarily applies to the Confederate statues, which became a subject of debate with the rise of the Civil Rights Movement. Modern civil rights organizations argue that these monuments are a reminder of events that continue to have devastating consequences for African-American communities. While the fight to remove, or at least rename, the Confederate monuments has lasted for several decades, over the past years, the controversies rose to the point that in 2021, over 70 of them were removed from their positions. Claiming that they represent an enduring legacy of hate and violence, civil rights activists continue to rally for removing more Confederate monuments, thus leaving the future of the remaining 723 that are still standing as memorials for some of the most consequential battles and heroic deeds uncertain. In addition to the individual monuments, there are 741 roadways, over 200 schools, 51 buildings, 38 parks, and 22 holidays commemorating the legacy of the Confederacy. Beyond representing the consolidation of the infamous "Lost Cause" ideology, another argument used against the Confederate monuments is that, unlike Union markers and monuments, these were built immediately after the war ended. By the time they were commissioned, a violent restoration of White supremacy was on the rise in the South; hence, the Confederate monuments had a distinctively racial context and, according to many, couldn't be considered parts of the American heritage.

The Link between the Civil War and the Modern Civil Rights Movement

Reaching back to the era before the Civil War, the modern civil rights movement encompasses a 400-year legacy of American history punctuated by racism, White supremacy, slavery, and social, political, and economic discrimination.

Ever since some states began to abolish slavery after the Revolutionary War, White Americans were divided on how to build a post-slavery society. As a result, issues like targeting free Black people in discriminatory treatment and suggestions that they should leave the country arose. The first civil rights movement was born to challenge and transform these controversial ideas and resolve the issues they caused, helping to build a multiracial society. However, as these notions were just as controversial as the ones they aimed to demolish, they laid the foundations for centuries of struggles to come.

After the Civil War, the Reconstruction era began, giving hope that the inequities of slavery and its economic, social, and political legacy would finally be redressed. During the Reconstruction, political and economic leaders also aimed to solve the issue that arose from the readmission of the 11 states that seceded from the Union before or at the war's outbreak. However, by 1877, it became evident that all attempts to resolve the proposed issues failed. While the reconstruction gave way to the 13th, 14th, and 15th amendments, which meant to provide voting and legal rights to former slaves and their descendants, these were only enforced initially. After the Federal troops left the South, White supremacy arose, and the voting rights of African Americans were once again suppressed. Those who wanted to vote had to pay a poll tax and pass a literacy test, neither of which was possible for many of the former slaves. Even worse, an elaborate system of segregation was created, which was buttressed by the ruling of the U.S. Supreme Court in the Plessy vs. Ferguson case in 1896. Essentially offering a constitutional basis for legal segregation, the ruling led to many challenges to all the systems it supported, not to mention the protests of early civil rights activists.

With their rights denied, many African Americans in the South failed to thrive economically, and many families in rural communities were forced into signing so-called "sharecropping agreements," which were another form of slavery. They were given loans, which they were unable to pay back, amassing debts ("debt slavery" was another term used for these agreements.

The modern civil rights movement began in the late 1950s, and during the 1960s, it slowly restored the previously withheld African American rights. Thanks to the relentless work of the Black activists of the '60s civil rights movement, African Americans now have the right to vote and began to reclaim the rights they had been seeking since (and even before) the end of the American Civil War. Despite the opening they gained after the Civil War, the movement took time to build, and after its landmark success on working rights, it seemed to slow down. However, in recent years, the contemporary civil rights movement has begun to win some of the biggest battles in American history – an analogy to the Civil War's events.

Shaping America's National Identity

Historians, veterans, and civilians who take time to study the American Civil War agree that this was one of the most transformative events in American history. The country that was a shaky union of rural communities forming the states was transformed into a powerful, modern country with a thriving economy and industrial advancements. In other words, it rose from an insignificant country to one of the most prominent world powers (as it became known during the World Wars).

From changes in the economy to the role of the federal government, the Civil War brought on many new features that shaped the American national identity. One of the most prominent factors that changed the country's role in the world was the transformation of core beliefs about rights, citizenship, and democracy. With pride being replaced with doubts about the system before the Civil War and the growing dissatisfaction with the definition of American people with American rights, the changes were inevitable. The war brought controversial consequences to some of the most deep-rooted American values, but once their roots were planted, their transformative effects rose. Some of the beliefs around national identity that were changed pertain to democracy. The war for abolishing slavery spiked the question of who gets to vote. For centuries, many Americans believed that only a select group (namely, White men) could participate in democracy. They also argued that the former slaves should be granted the rights and immunity that came with American citizenship. Others had contrasting opinions on both matters. Beliefs about the country's role in the world were also divided. Before the Civil War, women and enslaved African Americans in the South were not allowed to vote; however, afterward, the 15th Amendment granted the former slave men voting rights.

Before the Civil War, the right to American citizenship was limited to White men and women, as well as free African Americans in the Northern states (and even they had limitations depending on their state of residence). Even Irish and German immigrants and the Mexicans living on the territories acquired by the Mexican war were granted citizenship before enslaved African Americans and Native Americans. The slaves in the South were considered property and not people; therefore, they couldn't become citizens. By contrast, the enactment of the 13th Amendment, shortly after the war's end, abolished slavery, and the former slaves ceased to be property. The following 14th Amendment declared that anyone born in the United States or who became naturalized after immigration would be granted citizenship. While both citizenship and voting rights of the former slaves were temporarily revoked in the Segregation Era, they would gain them back as the beliefs around national identity were reshaped once again.

When it comes to beliefs about the role and relation of the United States toward the world abroad, the changes were just as radical. While trying to isolate itself to prevent potential entanglements with more powerful forces, the practices of conquest and occupation, using the idea of divine manifestation across the continent, led to conflicts with neighboring countries, beginning with Mexico. These practices continued even after the Civil War, but some ended with World War I when the United States officially abandoned isolationism as a foreign policy. On the other hand, the initial drive to expand borders toward the Pacific became even greater.

While some changes were slower to come and others were shifted back and forth, the transformative power of the Civil War on national identity is undeniable. When comparing the period between 1844 and 1877, there was a big expansion in ideology that allowed the former slaves of the South to gain voting rights and citizenship. While these were lost again until the 1960s (at least in practice, as they were still present on paper), they were regained by the efforts of those inspired by the ideology brought on by the Civil War a century before. People rallied against transferring voting rights and citizenship from a paper trail into real life.

Recognizing these transformative aspects of the American Civil War enables the American nation to appreciate the complexity of this period and its far-reaching influence on the future course of the nation's history and identity.

The Influence of Civil War Military Tactics and Innovations on Modern Warfare

"MERRIMAC" IN DRY DOCK, BEING CONVERTED INTO
THE IRON BATTERY "VIRGINIA."

Besides the innovative strategies employed by military leaders in the Civil War, the era was also
marked by prominent technological advancements.
*https://commons.wikimedia.org/wiki/File:MERRIMAC_in_dry_dock,_being_converted_into_th
e_iron_Battery_VIRGINIA_LCCN2004671787.jpg*

While many view it as a remarkable chapter in American history, the Civil War taught people much more than how the predecessors faced political, economic, and societal changes. It holds valuable lessons about warfare, much of which was implemented in the development of later military tactics and innovations. Besides the innovative strategies employed by military leaders in the Civil War, the era was also marked by prominent technological advancements. One of the most transformative effects was seen in land warfare, which was fascinated by the railroads that allowed for the quick advancement of troops. Rifling in the artillery and small arms was another tactic first introduced during the Civil War. Coupled with new methods for fortifying fields, bases, and trenches, the new arms techniques made battles easier to fight.

Heavily fortified with iron elements, warships like the CSS Virginia and the USS Monitor took the Civil War sea battles and those that followed to a whole new level. Gone were the days of vulnerable wooden naval vessels. Moreover, the introduction of submarines and the invention of naval torpedoes and mines during this war represent yet another leap in warfare technology.

Rapid communication during the Civil War was facilitated by telegraphy, enabling swift relay of orders and setting precedence for future warfare situations where rapid communication would be of vital importance. All of these innovations shaped the developing military strategies of the United States and many other countries that took on the task of learning from this monumental pivot toward modernizing warfare.

Rooted in deep causes tied to societal and ideological divisions and marked by progression, the American Civil War was an event with long-lasting effects on warfare strategy development. A unique concept introduced by the war was the Total War, which led to significant technological innovations and launched a new era of remarkable societal transformation. The causes, events, and legacy of this war changed the nation's warfare, challenging military leaders to come up with new tactics and innovations in order to rise as victors in future battles.

The Portrayal of the Civil War in Art and Culture

In the little over 150 years after its spike, the Civil War played a crucial role in art and culture, capturing artists' imaginations and inspiring much-appreciated pieces. When it comes to popular culture, two prominent features of the Civil War were seen in the movies *Django Unchained* and *Lincoln*, both of which were massively successful, albeit somewhat controversial. Beyond this, museums and artists across the country feature and create pieces that commemorate, re-envision, and often deconstruct the war's legacies. Rather than following the chronological events, contemporary depictions of the war either try to highlight individual achievements or focus on transforming educational material into art.

Initially, after the war, it was believed that the events and effects of the Civil War mattered only to some artists (like the ones commissioned to create markers and monuments. However, in contemporary culture, this view is seen as false as art historians have proven that all American artists were impacted and influenced by the events of the Civil War. In the early works, artists often expressed their views on the causes of the war through landscape designs, as seen in paintings like Frederic Edwin Church's *Meteor of 1860* and Martin Johnson Heade's *Approaching Thunder Storm,* both dating a year or two before the Civil War, but during times when tensions were high and about to reach the boiling point. These landscape designs are now translated as emotional rollercoasters that people in the era were subjected to.

After the war broke out, there was a shift toward depicting battlefields in their true light – as the scenes of vicious and bloody battles – as opposed to the picturesque scenes people associated with chivalry from romantic tales. This depiction was particularly featured in photography, which fascinated the public and caused much grief to the nation.

Still, the portrayals at the beginning of the era only showed one side of the story. Telling the tale of the African heritage and struggle was the job of artists yet to come. Nowadays, exhibitions and narratives (including audio and video sources from personal accounts) in institutions like the Museum of the African Diaspora showcase stories of the courage and fight of African Americans during and after the Civil War. These offer the opportunity to move beyond the one-dimensional account of slavery and enslavement, highlighting the importance of abolishing the practice.

Contemporary artists like Kara Walker, Fred Wilson, and Barnaby Furnas offer even deeper insights into the stereotypes on both sides with their renditions of the Civil War and the Reconstruction. Other artists choose to focus on reenactments of art pieces created during and shortly after the war. For example, Thomas Moran's 1862 painting, called *Slave Hunt, Dismal Swamp, Virginia,* showcasing a slave family escaping from their hunters, was reimagined by Whitfield Lovell in 2002, now depicting the slaves as dignified working people and homesteaders.

Conclusion

The American Civil War resolved the identity crisis that the nation experienced following the American Revolution and the drafting of the Constitution. First, it determined how the Constitution would be interpreted, and second, it established America as a united nation. In the past, the "United States" was used as a plural noun to collectively refer to the many states that made up the nation. However, the Civil War reframed what the United States meant in the mind of the populace by solidifying it as a singular noun describing a nation.

The deadly Civil War shook the nation at its foundation. 620,000 soldiers died in the conflict, which was a total of 2% of the population. To put this into perspective, if 2% of the population were killed in battle today, that would be over six million people. The massive bloodshed was like the water of the country breaking to birth a new nation. The sectionalism of the past was gradually reduced following the Civil War. Instead of people identifying more with their Southern or Northern heritage, they are cleaved to their identity as Americans. The balance between states' rights and federal governance is more stable today as a consequence of the outcome of the Civil War. Those who promoted disunity were defeated, giving way to a system that is representative of the collective while acknowledging that the Constitution allows states to determine their destiny with the boundaries created by the outcomes of the war.

The economic destiny of the country was also defined at the end of the Civil War. The slavery-based economy of the South lost out to the industrialism of the North, which gave birth to the free market capitalism that made the United States so prosperous. The ship of the nation got steered into the seas of modernity, taking the country out of an agrarian focus and into the technological future that the globalized world participates in today.

The beginnings of the nation's ideology of freedom, justice, and equality were established following the war. The freedom of slaves took African Americans one step closer to being full citizens who participated in the direction of the country. What began at the end of the Civil War culminated in the election of Barack Obama in 2008 as the first Black president of the United States. The abolition of slavery started the long battle for the civil rights of Black people that, to some extent, continues today.

The details of the Civil War will keep being repeated in popular media and school textbooks because it hits so close to the heart of what it means to be American socially, politically, culturally, and economically. Exploring the stories of the war reminds Americans how the country got to the privileged position it holds in the world today. The horrors and triumphs of the brave people who fought for the country's soul planted the seeds that now bear the fruits of freedom.

Check out another book in the series

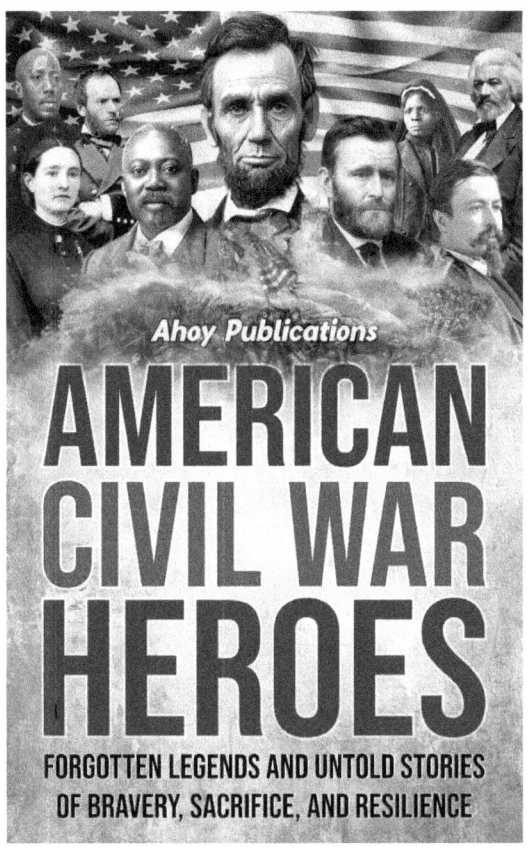

References

admin. (2023, June 6). What Makes the American Civil War Unique. Battlefield Tours of Virginia. https://battlefieldtoursofvirginia.com/what-makes-the-american-civil-war-unique-in-history/

Allen, T. (2007). Intelligence in the civil war. Federation of American Scientists. https://irp.fas.org/cia/product/civilwar.pdf

American Battlefield Trust. (n.d.). Harriet Beecher Stowe. American Battlefield Trust. https://www.battlefields.org/learn/biographies/harriet-beecher-stowe

American Battlefield Trust. (2017, August 29). 10 Facts: Civil War Battlefield Monuments, Markers, and Tablets. American Battlefield Trust. https://www.battlefields.org/learn/articles/10-facts-civil-war-battlefield-monuments-markers-and-tablets

American Battlefield Trust. (2018a, March 7). 10 Facts: What Everyone Should Know About the Civil War. American Battlefield Trust. https://www.battlefields.org/learn/articles/10-facts-what-everyone-should-know-about-civil-war

American Battlefield Trust. (2018b, April 6). Battle of Shiloh Facts & Summary. American Battlefield Trust. https://www.battlefields.org/learn/civil-war/battles/shiloh

American Battlefield Trust. (2023, March 29). Spy Executions During the American Civil War. American Battlefield Trust. https://www.battlefields.org/learn/articles/spy-executions-during-american-civil-war

American Red Cross. (2018). Clara Barton. American Red Cross. https://www.redcross.org/about-us/who-we-are/history/clara-barton.html

America's Legacy Links. (n.d.). Clara Barton. America's Legacy Links. http://www.americaslegacylinks.com/clara_barton.html

Ancestral Findings. (2019, September 25). Andre Cailloux: Unsung Heroes of the Civil War. Ancestral Findings. https://ancestralfindings.com/andre-cailloux-unsung-heroes-of-the-civil-war/

Andrews, E. (2019, January 31). 5 Daring Slave Escapes. HISTORY. https://www.history.com/news/5-daring-slave-escapes

Arlington Public Library. (2020, March 19). Angel of the Battlefield: Humanitarian Clara Barton. Library.arlingtonva.us. https://library.arlingtonva.us/2020/03/19/angel-of-the-battlefield-humanitarian-clara-barton/

Balkansky, A. (2020, June 16). Harriet Tubman: Conductor on the Underground Railroad | Headlines and Heroes. Blogs.loc.gov. https://blogs.loc.gov/headlinesandheroes/2020/06/harriet-tubman-conductor-on-the-underground-railroad/

Biography. (2022, October 7). Henry "Box" Brown - Facts, Magician & Life. Biography. https://www.biography.com/activists/henry-box-brown

Blanton, D. (2017, December 7). Women Soldiers of the Civil War. National Archives. https://www.archives.gov/publications/prologue/1993/spring/women-in-the-civil-war-1.html

Blight, D. W., & Max-o-matic. (2022, December 21). Was the Civil War Inevitable? The New York Times. https://www.nytimes.com/2022/12/21/magazine/civil-war-jan-6.html

Bolick, K. (2021, December). Clara Barton Epitomized the Heroism of Nurses. Smithsonian Magazine. https://www.smithsonianmag.com/history/clara-barton-hero-nurse-180979006/

Boot, A. (n.d.). Civil War. Women & the American Story. https://wams.nyhistory.org/a-nation-divided/civil-war/

Bryant, T. (n.d.). University of Delaware Research. Www1.Udel.edu. http://www1.udel.edu/researchmagazine/issue/vol2_no2_security/escape_from_fort_delaware.html

Carnahan, B. M. (2019). StackPath. Essentialcivilwarcurriculum.com. https://www.essentialcivilwarcurriculum.com/espionage.html

Carson, A. (2021). Bureau of Justice Statistics · Statistical Tables. https://bjs.ojp.gov/content/pub/pdf/msfp0119st.pdf

Clement, N. (2022, February 18). Harriet Tubman: A Transformational Leader. St. Cloud Technical Community College. https://sctcc.edu/news/02-18-2022/harriet-tubman-transformational-leader

Connors, T. (2008, February 29). How the Underground Railroad Worked. HowStuffWorks. https://history.howstuffworks.com/historical-events/underground-railroad.htm

Cox, K. L. (2021, January 14). Perspective | Five myths about the Lost Cause. Washington Post. https://www.washingtonpost.com/outlook/five-myths/five-myths-about-the-lost-cause/2021/01/14/78853464-55f9-11eb-a08b-f1381ef3d207_story.html

De Witte, M. (2020, July 16). Why Confederate monuments are coming down now. Stanford News. https://news.stanford.edu/2020/07/16/confederate-monuments-coming-now/

Deily-Swearingen, S. (n.d.). StackPath. Www.essentialcivilwarcurriculum.com. https://www.essentialcivilwarcurriculum.com/sectionalism.html

Doyle, J. H. (2015, June 30). The Civil War Was Won By Immigrant Soldiers | Essay | Zócalo Public Square. Zócalo Public Square. https://www.zocalopublicsquare.org/2015/06/30/the-civil-war-was-won-by-immigrant-soldiers/chronicles/who-we-were/

Edmonds, M. (2014, October 8). Frederick Douglass's Narrative: Myth of the Happy Slave. NEH-Edsitement. https://edsitement.neh.gov/lesson-plans/frederick-douglasss-narrative-myth-happy-slave

Encyclopedia Virginia. (n.d.). Brown, Henry Box (1815 or 1816–1897) – Encyclopedia Virginia. Encyclopedia Virginia. https://encyclopediavirginia.org/entries/brown-henry-box-1815-or-1816-1897/

Equal Justice Initiative. (2020). Reconstruction in America | EJI Report. EJI Reports. https://eji.org/report/reconstruction-in-america/

Evans, F. (2021, February 3). Reconstruction: A Timeline of the Post-Civil War Era. History. https://www.history.com/news/reconstruction-timeline-steps

Faust, D. (2019). Death and Dying–Civil War Era National Cemeteries: Discover Our Shared Heritage Travel Itinerary. Nps.gov. https://www.nps.gov/nr/travel/national_cemeteries/death.html

Flavion, G. (2018, July 11). Civil War Prison Camps. American Battlefield Trust. https://www.battlefields.org/learn/articles/civil-war-prison-camps

Giselle Rhoden and Dalila Paul. (2022, February 3). 73 confederate monuments were removed or renamed last year, report finds. CNN. https://www.cnn.com/2022/02/02/us/confederate-monuments-removed-2021-whose-heritage/index.html

GovInfo. (2019, March 25). Susan B. Anthony, Icon of the Women's Suffrage Movement | govinfo. Govinfo.gov. https://www.govinfo.gov/features/susan-b-anthony

Grant, T. K. (2022, January 31). The Underground Railroad. History. https://kids.nationalgeographic.com/history/article/the-underground-railroad

Greenspan, J. (2019, February 8). 8 Key Contributors to the Underground Railroad. HISTORY. https://www.history.com/news/8-key-contributors-to-the-underground-railroad

Gross, J. (2008). War Crimes Against Southern Civilians. Civil War Book Review, 10(1). https://repository.lsu.edu/cgi/viewcontent.cgi?article=2690&context=cwbr

Gudmestad, R. (2019, December 3). Faith made Harriet Tubman fearless as she rescued slaves. The Conversation. http://theconversation.com/faith-made-harriet-tubman-fearless-as-she-rescued-slaves-127592

Harriet Beecher Stowe Center. (2018). Harriet Beecher Stowe. Harriet Beecher Stowe Center. https://www.harrietbeecherstowecenter.org/harriet-beecher-stowe/harriet-beecher-stowe-life/

Hayward, N. (2018). Susan B. Anthony. National Women's History Museum. https://www.womenshistory.org/education-resources/biographies/susan-b-anthony

History of American Women. (2013, July 18). Diaries of Civil War Nurses. History of American Women. https://www.womenhistoryblog.com/2013/07/diaries-of-civil-war-nurses.html

HISTORY.COM. (2023, April 24). Reconstruction. History.com. https://www.history.com/topics/american-civil-war/reconstruction

History.com. (2009, October 29). Sojourner Truth. HISTORY.com. https://www.history.com/topics/black-history/sojourner-truth

History.com. (2018a, August 21). Battle of Wilson's Creek - Winner, Facts, Civil War. HISTORY. https://www.history.com/topics/american-civil-war/battle-of-wilsons-creek

History.com. (2018b, September 3). Secret Agents in Hoop Skirts: Women Spies of the Civil War. HISTORY. https://www.history.com/news/secret-agents-in-hoop-skirts-women-spies-of-the-civil-war

History.com. (2018c, September 4). Emancipation Proclamation. HISTORY. https://www.history.com/topics/american-civil-war/emancipation-proclamation

History.com. (2018d, September 11). Stonewall Jackson - Death, Accomplishments, General. HISTORY. https://www.history.com/topics/american-civil-war/stonewall-jackson

History.com. (2018e, October 2). Battle of Antietam. HISTORY. https://www.history.com/topics/american-civil-war/battle-of-antietam

History.com. (2019a, February 7). Harriet Beecher Stowe. HISTORY. https://www.history.com/topics/american-civil-war/harriet-beecher-stowe

History.com. (2019b, February 8). Spying in the Civil War. HISTORY. https://www.history.com/topics/american-civil-war/civil-war-spies

History.com. (2019c, February 8). Women in the Civil War. HISTORY. https://www.history.com/topics/american-civil-war/women-in-the-civil-war

History.com. (2019d, December 11). First Battle of Bull Run - Dates, Location & Who Won. HISTORY. https://www.history.com/topics/american-civil-war/first-battle-of-bull-run

History.com. (2023a, March 29). Harriet Tubman. History.com. https://www.history.com/topics/black-history/harriet-tubman

History.com. (2023b, March 29). Underground Railroad. History. https://www.history.com/topics/black-history/underground-railroad

History.com. (2023c, April 20). Civil War. HISTORY.com. https://www.history.com/topics/american-civil-war/american-civil-war-history

Intelligence. (n.d.). INTEL - Confederate Espionage. Www.intelligence.gov. https://www.intelligence.gov/evolution-of-espionage/civil-war/confederate-espionage

James Billingslea Mitchell - Biographies - The Civil War in America | Exhibitions - Library of Congress. (2012, November 12). Www.loc.gov. https://www.loc.gov/exhibits/civil-war-in-america/biographies/james-billingslea-mitchell.html

Janowski, D. (2022). Elmira Prison Camp. Chemung History. https://www.chemunghistory.com/elmira-prison-camp

John F. Kennedy Presidential Library and Museum. (2000). Civil Rights Movement. Jfklibrary.org. https://www.jfklibrary.org/learn/about-jfk/jfk-in-history/civil-rights-movement

Karamanski, T. J. (2020). Camp Douglas. Chicagohistory.org. http://www.encyclopedia.chicagohistory.org/pages/207.html

Kerrigan, E. (2018, April 18). Learning from History: Harriet Tubman and Leadership. Integris Performance Advisors. https://integrispa.com/learning-from-history-harriet-tubman-and-leadership/

Khan Academy. (2018). Comparing the effects of the Civil War on American national identity. Khan Academy. https://www.khanacademy.org/humanities/us-history/civil-war-era/reconstruction/v/comparing-the-effects-of-the-civil-war-on-american-national-identity

Kulke, S. (2022, May 10). Tracing the American civil rights movement that started long before the Civil War. News.northwestern.edu. https://news.northwestern.edu/stories/2021/04/kate-masur-until-justice-be-done/

Lee, S. (2017). Healing Without Supplies: Confederate Medical Care for Prisoners of War – Virginia Center for Civil War Studies. Civilwar.vt.edu. https://civilwar.vt.edu/healing-without-supplies-confederate-medical-care-for-prisoners-of-war/

Library of Congress. (n.d.-a). African American Spirituals. Library of Congress, Washington, D.C. 20540 USA. https://www.loc.gov/item/ihas.200197495/#:~:text=As%20Africanized%20Christianity%20took%20hold

Library of Congress. (n.d.-b). Civil War and Reconstruction, 1861-1877 | U.S. History Primary Source Timeline | Classroom Materials | Library of Congress. Library of Congress, Washington, D.C. 20540 USA. https://www.loc.gov/classroom-materials/united-states-history-primary-source-timeline/civil-war-and-reconstruction-1861-1877/

Library of Congress. (n.d.-c). Image 1 of [William Augustus Bowles]. Library of Congress, Washington, D.C. 20540 USA. https://www.loc.gov/resource/wpalh3.32050510/?st=pdf&pdfPage=1

Library of Congress. (2012). April 1861–April 1862 - The Civil War in America | Exhibitions - Library of Congress. Loc.gov. https://www.loc.gov/exhibits/civil-war-in-america/april-1861-april-1862.html

Library of Congress. (2019). Reconstruction and its Aftermath - The African American Odyssey: A Quest for Full Citizenship | Exhibitions (Library of Congress). Loc.gov. https://www.loc.gov/exhibits/african-american-odyssey/reconstruction.html

Library of Congress. (2020). April 1862–November 1862 - The Civil War in America | Exhibitions - Library of Congress. Loc.gov. https://www.loc.gov/exhibits/civil-war-in-america/april-1862-november-1862.html

Little, B. (2021, November 1). How the US Civil War Inspired Women to Enter Nursing. HISTORY. https://www.history.com/news/nursing-women-civil-war

Lloyd Sealy Library. (2019a). LibGuides: American History: The Civil War and Reconstruction: Aftermath of the Civil War. Cuny.edu. https://guides.lib.jjay.cuny.edu/c.php?g=288398&p=4496620

Lloyd Sealy Library. (2019b). LibGuides: American History: The Civil War and Reconstruction: Buildup to the Civil War. Cuny.edu. https://guides.lib.jjay.cuny.edu/c.php?g=288398&p=4496530

Lumen. (n.d.). Fighting in 1862 | United States History I. Courses.lumenlearning.com. https://courses.lumenlearning.com/wm-ushistory1/chapter/fighting-in-1862/

Marker, J. (2019, August 15). The Spies Behind Lincoln's "Secret War to Save a Nation." National Archives. https://www.archives.gov/news/articles/douglas-waller-lincolns-spies-civil-war

McCormick, J. (2018, March 24). The Most Effective Female Spies of the American Civil War | War History Online. War History Online. https://www.warhistoryonline.com/american-civil-war/effective-female-spies-civil-war.html

McPherson, J. (2017, December 15). Out of War, a New Nation. National Archives. https://www.archives.gov/publications/prologue/2010/spring/newnation.html

Michals, D. (2015a). Harriet Tubman. National Women's History Museum. https://www.womenshistory.org/education-resources/biographies/harriet-tubman

Michals, D. (2015b). Sojourner Truth. National Women's History Museum. https://www.womenshistory.org/education-resources/biographies/sojourner-truth

Michals, D. (2017). Harriet Beecher Stowe. National Women's History Museum. https://www.womenshistory.org/education-resources/biographies/harriet-beecher-stowe

Mobley, T. (2021, December 10). The Tale of Two White Houses: Espionage during the Civil War. White House History. https://www.whitehousehistory.org/the-tale-of-two-white-houses-espionage-during-the-civil-war

Muchowski, K. (2019, January 19). Civil War Recruitment. Encyclopedia of Arkansas. https://encyclopediaofarkansas.net/entries/civil-war-recruitment-6391/

Munoz, J. (2021, June 19). Top 10 Chilling Civil War Stories. Listverse. https://listverse.com/2021/06/19/top-10-chilling-civil-war-stories/

Mwewa, M. (2023a, April 24). Life on the Battlefield: Soldiers' Stories from the Civil War. Kinnu. https://kinnu.xyz/kinnuverse/history/american-civil-war/life-on-the-battlefield-soldiers-stories-from-the-civil-war/

Mwewa, M. (2023b, April 24). The War at Home: How the Civil War Affected Civilians. Kinnu. https://kinnu.xyz/kinnuverse/history/american-civil-war/the-war-at-home-how-the-civil-war-affected-civilians/

National Archives. (2018, January 5). The Emancipation Proclamation. National Archives. https://www.archives.gov/exhibits/featured-documents/emancipation-proclamation

National Geographic. (2022, May 20). The Underground Railroad | National Geographic Society. Education.nationalgeographic.org. https://education.nationalgeographic.org/resource/underground-railroad/

National Geographic Society. (2022, June 2). Defining Battles of the Civil War | National Geographic Society. Education.nationalgeographic.org. https://education.nationalgeographic.org/resource/defining-battles-civil-war

National Museum of African American History and Culture. (n.d.). 13th Amendment to the U.S. Constitution is Passed. National Museum of African American History and Culture. https://nmaahc.si.edu/explore/stories/13th-amendment-us-constitution-passed

National Museum of Civil War Medicine. (2016, January 14). Clara Barton-Civil War Medicine Museum. National Museum of Civil War Medicine. https://www.civilwarmed.org/clarabarton/

National Park Service. (2016). Successful Escapes From Andersonville - Andersonville National Historic Site (U.S. National Park Service). Nps.gov. https://www.nps.gov/ande/learn/historyculture/escapefromandersonville.htm

National Park Service. (2017). Antietam: Letters and Diaries of Soldiers and Civilians - Antietam National Battlefield (U.S. National Park Service). Nps.gov. https://www.nps.gov/anti/learn/education/classrooms/antietam-letters-and-diaries-of-soldiers-and-civilians.htm

National Park Service. (2020, October 15). What is the Underground Railroad? - Underground Railroad (U.S. National Park Service). Nps.gov. https://www.nps.gov/subjects/undergroundrailroad/what-is-the-underground-railroad.htm

National Park Service. (2021, April 12). Dr. Mary Edwards Walker (U.S. National Park Service). Nps.gov. https://www.nps.gov/people/mary-walker.htm

National Park Service. (2022, October 31). Preserving Places of Captivity: Civil War Prisons in the National Parks - Andersonville National Historic Site (U.S. National Park Service). Www.nps.gov. https://www.nps.gov/ande/learn/historyculture/civil-war-prisons-in-the-national-parks.htm

Norwood, A. R. (2017). Louisa May Alcott. National Women's History Museum. https://www.womenshistory.org/education-resources/biographies/louisa-may-alcott

Pathways to Freedom. (n.d.). Pathways to Freedom | About the Underground Railroad. Pathways.thinkport.org. https://pathways.thinkport.org/about/about9.cfm

PBS. (n.d.). Africans in America/Part 4/Narrative: Antebellum Slavery. Pbs.org. https://www.pbs.org/wgbh/aia/part4/4narr1.html

PBS. (2017). 7 Surprising Facts About Louisa May Alcott | MASTERPIECE. Masterpiece. https://www.pbs.org/wgbh/masterpiece/specialfeatures/little-women-7-surprising-facts-about-louisa-may-alcott/

PBS. (2019). Kids in the Civil War | American Experience | PBS. Pbs.org. https://www.pbs.org/wgbh/americanexperience/features/grant-kids/

PBS. (2022). Ely Parker 1844-1865. Pbs.org. https://www.pbs.org/warrior/content/timeline/opendoor/civilwarDiaries.html

Pollack, B. (2013, May 15). The Civil War in Art, Then and Now. ARTnews.com. https://www.artnews.com/art-news/news/the-civil-war-in-art-then-and-now-2223/

Rodgers, T. E. (2020, December 7). Hoosier Soldiers in the Civil War. IHB. https://www.in.gov/history/about-indiana-history-and-trivia/annual-commemorations/civil-war-150th/hoosier-voices-now/hoosier-soldiers-in-the-civil-war/

Román, I. (2020, November 10). 6 Black Heroes of the Civil War. HISTORY. https://www.history.com/news/black-heroes-us-civil-war-tubman-douglass-augusta-smalls-galloway

Smithsonian Magazine. (2011, May 9). Women Spies of the Civil War. Smithsonian Magazine. https://www.smithsonianmag.com/history/women-spies-of-the-civil-war-162202679/

Social Welfare. (2015, March 9). Emancipation Proclamation: January 1st, 1863. Social Welfare History Project. https://socialwelfare.library.vcu.edu/federal/emancipation-proclamation-1862/#:~:text=The%20South%20was%20furious%20over

Solowey, T. (2023, October 19). Civil War Camp Life | National Geographic Society. Education.nationalgeographic.org. https://education.nationalgeographic.org/resource/civil-war-camp-life

Tiverton Historical Society. (2022). A Tribute to Women Pioneers in Health Care. Tivertonhistorical.org. http://www.tivertonhistorical.org/tiverton-stories/a-tribute-to-women-pioneers-in-health-care/

U.S. Army Heritage and Education Center. (n.d.). Disease and Medical Care. U.S. Army Heritage and Education Center. https://ahec.armywarcollege.edu/exhibits/CivilWarImagery/cheney_disease.cfm

U.S. Army Heritage and Education Center. (2020). United States Sanitary Commission. Armywarcollege.edu. https://ahec.armywarcollege.edu/exhibits/CivilWarImagery/Sanitary_Commissionl.cfm

U.S. History. (n.d.). Canefight! Preston Brooks and Charles Sumner [ushistory.org]. U.S. History. https://www.ushistory.org/us/31e.asp

Underground Railroad. (n.d.). Routes – Underground Railroad. Underground Railroad. https://undergroundrailroad.org.uk/routes/

University Libraries. (2010). Federal Soldiers' Letters, 1861-1865; 1890. Unc.edu. https://finding-aids.lib.unc.edu/03185/

University of Rochester. (n.d.). Stanton/Anthony Friendship | The Susan B. Anthony Center. Www.rochester.edu.

Women's Rights National Historical Park. (2017, November 17). Sojourner Truth: Ain't I A Woman? Nps.gov. https://www.nps.gov/articles/sojourner-truth.htm

Wright, A. A. (2020, December 7). Women during the Civil War – Encyclopedia Virginia. Encyclopedia Virginia. https://encyclopediavirginia.org/entries/women-during-the-civil-war/

Zombek, A. M. (2020, December 7). Libby Prison – Encyclopedia Virginia. Encyclopedia Virginia. https://encyclopediavirginia.org/entries/libby-prison/

www.ingramcontent.com/pod-product-compliance
Lightning Source LLC
Chambersburg PA
CBHW070722130626
46553CB00005B/2108